HOME:
A Year of Miracles

by
James H. Kurt

© 2021 James H. Kurt. All rights reserved.

Children of Light Publications
02/02/2021

jameshkurt@gmail.com

ISBN: 978-1-7332154-8-0

No part of this book may be reproduced, stored in a retrieval system, or transmitted by any means without the written permission of the author.

Proofreading Assistance: Louis Guerriero

Cover photo/art by James Kurt.

Author's Website:
www.writingsofjameskurt.org

Podcasting Site:
www.hermitinthecity.libsyn.com

"Living by Christ's Blood,
We know all things are possible.
Living by Christ's Blood,
We see all things are new.
Living by Christ's Blood,
We are living in a miracle.

We are living in a miracle,
Living in a miracle,
Living by Christ's Blood."

final lyrics of "Miracle", from *Listening to the Lamp*,
ninth album of *Songs for Children of Light*
© 1984, 2003 James H. Kurt

HOME

Seeking home, whether our ultimate home in Heaven or our home here on earth, our ears and eyes must be attuned to the signs, the blessings, the miracles that surround us day to day. In these we find our way home.

The LORD is speaking to us, in the silence, in the troubles, and in the mundane. We are living in a miracle, in His presence, always. By His blood we have been saved, and baptized in Him we discover His grace. He is our Home; His Kingdom is come.

This miracle is most evident in the holy sacrifice of the Mass, wherein He is present to us every day. Do our souls thirst for Him like the deer for running streams? Do we set aside all that keeps us from His presence and do all we can to be with Him? Are our ears and eyes open to His call? Nothing should keep us from the House of God, for in Him we indeed find our home. Let us be His tabernacles; let us be His Body on earth.

Here is recorded a year of days in search of our home.

November 2019

A Year of Miracles

November 9, 2019 – St. John Lateran

Had a dream of seeking a way home, walking and walking, then returning, asking directions, pursuing a bus.... At one point I seemed to have arrived home (rather suddenly) on the porch of my childhood house. But I soon noticed it wasn't. (Just looked like it at first.)

As I lay in bed after the dream, I was very disappointed in myself for not considering Jesus my home (or praying to Him for help) or ever looking for a church.

It wasn't until I was praying Morning Prayer before early Mass (had read the Office and the Mass readings the previous evening) that I realized how perfectly today's feast of St. John Lateran, the Pope's Cathedral, answered my search – the Church is my home here on earth, and the New Jerusalem my home in Heaven. The readings really struck me (into a meditative state) at Mass: the Temple, our body as a temple, zeal for the Father's House...

And this is the anniversary of my engagement to Sylvia, another home for me; and our marriage is dedicated to the Church.

How I pray I will set my heart on my heavenly home and not seek it in material places and things.

Come, New Jerusalem, descend upon us this feast day.

November 10 – Resurrection

End of All Souls Novena. Made it to cemetery a second time in these nine days, praying for my relatives.

Readings on the Resurrection – O the life of Heaven! Also read of two or three deathbed conversions. There *is* only one place, one home for us all.

HOME

November 11 – Sickness

Plagued somewhat by sickness – very dry skin, especially on calves, where sores have been present for years and aggravated by itching of late; also having difficulty sitting, working, or doing much of anything... I realize why the sick are called "patients." How very necessary that virtue is. And so if this teaches me a little patience, it will have been a great blessing. (But I do hope to improve tomorrow, for teaching, etc.)

Very poignant that the Bishops' meeting begins today, a day when the gospel proclaims the fate of those who lead little ones astray – worse than a millstone around the neck in the sea! At least they did vote for a thorough account of the latest scandal.

November 12 – Glorified

Lying in bed this morning I tried to imagine what it would be like to be perfectly whole, completely healthy. Thank God I have had no broken bones and no need of medicines, just a number of little things generally under control. But blessed would it be to have no more deviated septum (breathing freely), no more dry throat or skin, no more weakness in arms or legs or back....

The priest noted that the first reading from Wisdom is often used at funerals, that today is the feast of St. Josaphat the martyr, and that we need to pray for the dead. He said at the Resurrection our bodies will be glorified like Jesus' and would likewise be able to walk through walls. (Had tried to imagine such a glorified body this morning during prayer.)

In our home in Heaven, such will be our state. Praise God!

November 13 – Frozen

Record cold; remarkably frigid walking to church this morning. Have not felt the icy cold hit my face like that since leaving NJ eight years ago. (At this time am back in Jersey City for fall teaching assignment.) But a walk in the park later in the afternoon, after it had gotten ten degrees warmer, was almost pleasant.

Let us thank God for all things, for the cold and the heat, the frost and the chill and the will to praise Him!

This morning my wife and I noticed that the fish in the small pond in the church courtyard seemed to be frozen in place (though one or the other would occasionally move slightly), so after Mass and adoration I rang the office bell. I was quite surprised to learn that these fish (Koi) virtually hibernate. The pond doesn't completely freeze and they find warmth and oxygen toward the bottom... and move very little. One person thought that they find niches among the rocks, an idea I liked since it made them seem like hermits, but I found no substantiation for this.

November 14 - Impermanency

So the hockey team I watch (Tampa Bay Lightning), who have been on the road more than any other team and had just come from playing two games in Sweden, returned to their home rink tonight... and scored four goals in the first seven minutes. No place like home.

The question of home arises again as I watch the game in the home area of the team I root against - an area that was my own home for some fifty years, and to which I still return for months each year - and cheer for the team from the place that has been my principal home for the past eight years.

A geographical home can be a changeable thing, one that does not last forever, even on this earth... much less in Heaven.

And on this feast of St. Albert (patron of scientists) we learn how wisdom, too, falls short of permanency. As Aquinas said: "Human reason is very deficient in things concerning God."

November 15 – The Hermit

This morning alone in chapel praying the Stations, I felt as if I were at Bethlehem Hermitage in the woods, in the quiet, in the peace... Perhaps this sense was induced by the garden courtyard outside the door, the plants from there that had been carried indoors, or by the cold – but I felt a special kinship with these hermits here in the presence of the Lord and found a certain longing for the monastic (or eremitic) life.

The priest spoke in his homily about loss and how it prepares us for the ultimate loss in death, and so for the world to come. And is there anyone more attuned to loss (and gain) than the hermit? There is no one else so alone, and yet so close to God.

November 16 – The Child

Prayed the Rosary after work this afternoon in our (small) adoration chapel, where a husband and wife and their seven children were in attendance for over an hour. Before leaving I knelt in front of Jesus and prayed for the Church (as is my habit). Usually when I offer this prayer my attention is focused on the hierarchy, though I do include all members. But kneeling today amongst the children, I realized the primary importance of those at the bottom of the pyramid (as it were). I was especially filled with the spirit and life of a child.

Here is the Church most evident, in the family and in children. Here it is more present, more alive, than in popes and bishops and lay leaders. Here *is* the Church.

"Let the children come unto me, for of such is the Kingdom of Heaven." O may I never lose the innocent heart of a child!

November 17 – Baptism

Baptism of Matthew Vincent.

November 2019

We happen upon a baptism (again) at Mass this morning. During the homily on this Sunday toward the close of the Church year, when the gospel reflects the end times, the priest asks how dying can preserve our life. Eternal life is the answer, of course. And it is eternal life this child enters upon this day in a church of family and strangers, all members of the mystical Body of Christ.

May he always carry the light.

November 18 – The NAME

Yesterday in his homily the priest also asked what the Name of God is. I was surprised to hear the woman in front of me make an effort at speaking the Tetragrammaton (as I spoke this Silence). It turned out the woman was an adorer in our chapel whom I had known years ago and with whom I had shared my understanding of the NAME, as well as a copy of my book. This seemed more than coincidence, so today I worked on preparing the book for republishing with the (less expensive) company I found recently, and with whom I just published four other books (and am working on republishing a couple of others).

While still speaking about the NAME and the Father's love for us, the priest gave the example of a child he'd seen the day before safely at rest, at peace, in his father's arms. It was very reminiscent of Psalm 31, which is on the back of *YHWH: Order of the Divine NAME*.

November 19 – Small Class

Oral presentations with main (six-credit) class, a small group of twelve, with usually fewer in attendance. Because the class is so small, it has become more intimate and conversational than most. There has been a good amount of time to "stretch out," to focus on and discuss topics of interest and importance. Showed *Unplanned* a couple of weeks ago and the students really appreciated it. At least one had a change of heart, which led to a change of orientation for her (abortion) presentation today.

HOME

Had been concerned earlier in the semester as I realized I could really be the students' grandfather; but that led to a more conscious effort to relax and connect with them. It seems to have worked.

November 20 - Talents

Today we hear the gospel of the ten talents, which has always held significance for me, especially regarding my writings. It began with the composition of the ten albums of lyrics for *Songs for Children of Light* - five of which were written in a month (Feb. '84) as a gift from Heaven, with five more added over the next few months. That project, including music and dance and drama, I worked on for about seven years, during an intense, monastery-like, conversion period.

And today I completed the preparation and submission of two more books for republishing; since they will cost so much less, I will be better able to promote or produce fruit with them. Gearing up with renewed vigor for four events in the new year.

But hearing that "whoever has, more will be given," I must admit to being a little frightened by the gifts of God that may come. Perhaps this is why I have been satisfied not to pursue any kind of "success." But we must succeed in the Lord and not be afraid of His love. All in His hands.

November 21 - Presentation of Mary

O that we would all live in the Temple, as the Temple, as She!
O her innocence! O her blessed union with the Lord!

In the church of Holy Rosary we pray the Hail Mary in honor of our Mother, who would hold us in her arms like the Baby Jesus, and who is held in the arms of the Father.

"Did you not know that I must be in my Father's House?" And is she not the Father's House, within whom the Spirit dwells, who gives birth to the only Son? And is He not always with her? O that He might be always with us! Let us know such peace!

November 22 – Division

Zeal for the LORD's House consumes Jesus again today, and the Temple is rededicated in the Maccabean period... but of course it is the Body of Christ that is the LORD's Temple. And is there anything more disturbing to the Lord than to see His House divided, to see division plaguing His people? It is the devil's dream: to infect man with the same disobedient pride he has chosen, to see him fall to the depths as well.

And there has been such a plague at work in our pro-life ministry (in Florida) of late, though I have only been witness to it from a distance. Our prayers must rise up as one as we fill up what is lacking in the sufferings of Christ; for what else is the Body made but such suffering in union with our God? Let us take these pangs upon our backs and sense His sweet blood flowing through our veins.

November 23 – Loneliness

Last class with Chinese students (one more with the other); collecting final essays, tallying grades...

It was difficult to develop a line of communication with this class, something I'm usually able to do well. The class was large, but the main problem was they just didn't speak much. There was so much I would have liked to discuss, but who knows what would have been appropriate?

I did get a smile from one of the students as she left, the one who replied to my question regarding the one-child policy after class recently (when only six students remained). I asked what it was like to be where everyone is an only child. She thought deeply about it and said: "Lonely." So sad what man can do without God.

And the irony is that here in the U.S. that same loneliness pervades (as Mother Teresa made clear). For we have a self-imposed one-child policy not dissimilar to China. Those more than two children are looked down upon, shunned for their large families... and so joy is far from us as well.

November 24 – Feast

Christ the King Sunday, and sitting on my winter coat during Mass (a few inches higher than usual), I did feel as if I were seated on a throne, like Jesus sitting on His throne (reminiscent of His depiction as Pantocrator). He rules over all, and we are called to rule with Him... if only the darkness were purged from us and only light remained. We must be His children of light.

And today is also our Thanksgiving Sunday, since we will be traveling Thanksgiving Day. Feast with wife and sister-in-law, their two nieces and a family friend. A special time for sharing as family. We spoke particularly of the death of the nieces' father and of our friend's husband. Also, final visit to cemetery and my relatives there, still in this month of November.

Who can say where our home is - our final resting place, our family's arms, this house in this place or that house in that place...? Again, our only home is in Heaven, where all souls shall indeed be purified and share in the feast of our Savior.

November 25 – Anawim

I realized today it is the anawim that matter to God, like the widow in our gospel who put her two coins in the treasury. We have a few such souls in the chapel each day, people who are easy to look past (if not down upon). The priest and those who read or serve seem the important figures... but the humble souls who stay in the church praying before and after Mass, those whom many do not notice, whose names are not known - these are truly the ones the Lord looks upon with great love. They are His special children.

We visit one such soul after adoration today, an elderly Spanish woman suffering recently from a couple of operations. I am proud to say she is my friend, and I pray the Lord will look kindly upon me for being so.

November 26 – Dust

In the end all we make and do is dust, says the priest, interpreting our readings today (at the end of the Church year) on Daniel's interpretation of the king's dream of the rock crushing mighty kingdoms to dust and Jesus' speaking of the destruction of the Temple.

The same might be said for our bodies; and the past few mornings in speaking the Divine NAME (YHWH) before rising, I realize this practice is fulfilled in the laying down of our lives, of our bodies, even unto death. In this we find peace, the peace of Christ, the peace of everlasting life.

November 27 – Leaving

Packing up and getting ready to leave early in the morning, to travel from our one 'home' here in NJ, where we have been staying with my 80-year-old sister-in-law for a few months (and where I have been able to teach a couple of classes)... to our other, adopted, now more permanent 'home' in Florida, where we live with my 91-year-old mom. Where our home really is, I cannot say; we are, I suppose, technically homeless.

Ready to leave, it seems, though one day just follows the other and things pass so gradually, so steadily, that I hardly notice anymore. It is time to go; that is all I know.

I pray blessings upon those we leave here, and upon those to whom we come. (And they all wish us a safe journey. Amen.)

November 28 – Train

In transit. Auto train now our home. And at dinner we sit with a Catholic woman who grew up not far from our area in NJ, and who now lives in the next town over from us in Florida. And we are blessed with a very inspiring conversation on religious themes (pro-life, helping homeless, etc.). When she is up north, she

HOME

actually lives and works at a retreat house, which is my own ideal home. The providential hand of God is clearly at work.

And the train itself is something of a monastery, very quiet; and since there are not a lot of passengers (this Thanksgiving Day), each has his own separate pair of seats, including my wife and I.

November 29 – Blessed Travel

Safe travel. All went so smoothly, so blessedly, with our journey. First person we met, while praying Office of Readings in lounge car before 6 a.m. breakfast, stopped to tell us about her recent pilgrimage to the Holy Land. Another devout Catholic. Then we arrived and got our car so quickly, we had nearly two hours at the (Mary, Queen of the Universe) shrine before Mass for Confession, Stations, adoration... and there was no traffic on the ride home.

It is almost scary when things go so well; there is a fear of my inability to remain patient when things turn bad. May the Lord give me that patience which will enable me to be at home, with Him, wherever I am and however things go.

And now we are home in Sarasota with my mom (and aunt).

November 30 – St. Andrew

Last day of the Church year and St. Andrew's Feast. Trying to get settled back in the house, sometimes get confused where I am and what I should be doing, as I forget my routine in this place. Though I suppose it must be more difficult for our neighbors to know where they are: they spend five weeks here, then five weeks in England, back and forth continually. I definitely would not know where I was upon waking.

But how ready was Andrew (and Peter and John and James) immediately to leave his work and home to follow Jesus wherever He traveled, never having one place to lay his head. We should be so ready to leave all for Christ.

December 2019

December 1 – Advent

First day of Advent. One could say today: "Happy New Year!" for indeed the Church year begins with Advent. The apocalyptic readings of recent weeks change to those of hope for the coming of Christ, though also with a call to turn from our sins.

Visited two nursing homes and one house with the Sacrament... and dealing with my aunt's meds. I have visited nursing homes for twenty-five years, and often they are not like homes at all but more like jail cells. Some do accommodate residents well and try to inspire a familial sense... but they can certainly be sad places, where the end is always upon minds and hearts. But bless those who maintain hope, hope in a world to come when souls shall soar as on eagles' wings.

A new day is dawning. Let us be ready to welcome the Lord when He comes.

December 2 – Back Home

A couple of more home visits with the Sacrament. Repairing crucifix for Planned Parenthood witness tomorrow. A number of "welcome back"s from folks at daily Mass.

It does feel good to be home, to be back in Sarasota. Even seem to feel physically better. And returning to our places at PP should be a big step in our return home. It is there we are perhaps most called, where we are particularly at home, or at least in place (of witness). Though nothing can compare with being at home in church, it is mostly the presence of the Lord that matters there, and He is in *every* Catholic church.

Into the New Jerusalem let us come.

December 3 – Together

Despite the particularly cold weather (for Florida), it felt very good, very comfortable, to be back praying in front of Planned

HOME

Parenthood for an hour this morning (and giving other witness as well). May the Lord bless this work.

We must come as merest children, with complete trust in the Lord and trust in one another, and love even our enemies. It is He who accomplishes anything in us, and we cannot go it alone. All must work together, and as a whole and individually put all in God's hands, lest we become angry or anxious or frustrated... and work against His call, which is always to love. May He give us the grace to do so.

December 4 – The Way

Back to Luncheon for Life after three months away. Here is another home with loving family and friends, the Body of Christ working together for the cause of life.

Speaker confirmed thoughts above and emphasized how we must suffer for those in need, going into the well and getting our hands bloodied for those in desperate straits or far from the Lord. An exhortation, really, to love our enemy, to live the way of Jesus. This call is so important because in this work the enemy is so present, so real, in so many ways. Trust in God and His love is so necessary.

December 5 – Caregiving

Day of confusion centered around my aunt's problems with short-term memory. Missing meds, some found out of place... Later I must pack her clothes for her to keep her from increasing anxiety and tears as she readies to leave.... And my mother can hardly hear and seems unaware at times. It is rather like caring for children. I can't imagine the pressure upon full-time caregivers. I just don't know if I could do it, or where things will end up with my mom. Always thought we would keep her in the house, but I can see how things could get so bad there might be no other choice but some kind of home. I pray not, though, and thank God I am married to a nurse, one of those who are trained not to take it all too seriously. May God also help my cousins, as my aunt returns north tomorrow.

But Mass was a particular refuge today, especially after two days of communion services (diocesan priests on retreat).

December 6 – Family

Took aunt to the airport this evening, where we met her son; he then had to turn around and head back to NJ with her.

Family. Was very close to this cousin when we were kids. Spent five weeks together every summer down the shore – seven kids and two (or four) adults in a small, three-bedroom house. This place and this time have come to represent the joy of childhood and family life. I especially had a lot of fun with this cousin, since he was quite the comedian, picking up his sense of humor, he says, from my dad.

Tonight I made a good joke (about marriage) while we were conversing for a few moments, and he said he saw my father in me at that moment – even sort of framed my head with his hands in an animated manner.

Ahhh... the days of our youth, childhood joys – how close our family was then. Now just holding on to the vestiges of those days.

May we all reunite in Heaven.

December 7 – Jewish

Back to our Saturday posts at Planned Parenthood, addressing mainly clients seeking birth control on this non-abortion day. I must be a little rusty because it wasn't until the seventh (and last) car I encountered, just before leaving, that I was able to give out a brochure.

While standing at my post on a rather isolated block, I watch the birds and speak with those coming in and out of the rooming

HOME

house across the narrow street, a place generally for men a little down on their luck.

One gentleman upon seeing the Tetragrammaton hung upon my chest asked if I am Jewish. He said I looked it and was sure I had Semitic blood in my ancestry. I have often thought this, especially since I really don't know my history beyond grandparents on one side and great-grandparents on the other, both from countries (Poland and Germany) with significant Jewish populations.

Perhaps we all have Jewish blood in us from someone along the line. In the end all will at least be adopted sons of Israel.

December 8 – Serving the Lord

Sunday, so not Immaculate Conception (celebrated tomorrow).

Read at Mass, helped Knights afterward selling poinsettias for maternity home, then called friend suffering mental illness to see if he would be able to receive Communion.

Sometimes one thing follows another and I do feel I am serving the Lord; sometimes it seems there is not enough time to do everything I have to do. May all be done in God's time, not my own.

Today I manage to prep some podcasts for posting before heading out for parish Christmas party and then returning home to watch a film with my wife.

December 9 – Immaculate Conception

Praying during Mass today (some suffering from sickness upon me), saying to myself, realizing, I know nothing and can know nothing; and this truth leads to insight, prophetic insight wherein the Lord instructs one's soul. And I recall the sense I had when my wife and I were prayed over by a newly-ordained priest – a look into the time before light, when just the Spirit moved upon the waters... to the beginning of all and everything.

On this day we celebrate the Solemnity of the Immaculate Conception of Mary. How she looked into the heart of God; how she is united with the LORD in humility and purity... how she sees (and knows).

December 10 – Jersey City

Hundreds of shots fired in the streets of Jersey City just blocks from the college where I teach (where there is a lockdown), along the path I travel on my way home....

My poor hometown. What is it known for but violence? Perhaps the saddest thing is to hear residents say they are "used to gunshots," though not in the number that rang out today. How terrible to become used to violence, to take it in stride... though this episode certainly did shake everyone up.

In the streets of the New Jerusalem will be heard the sound of children playing. Old men and women will sit safely conversing. The lamb will lie down with the lion... Only peace on God's holy mountain.

December 11 – The Light Yoke

The first reading spoke of those who believe in the LORD never tiring but soaring as if on eagles' wings; and in the gospel Jesus invites us to take up His yoke and so find rest for our weary souls.

And quite remarkably, though before leaving for Mass I felt weak and wondered if perhaps I should not have fasted this morning as I fight off sickness... and though I had just been rushing from one task to another and found myself out of breath – as I prayed my Stations, I marveled at how much energy I suddenly had and how sickness had seemed to flee from me as I breathed deeply good health.

Let us indeed make our home beneath His Cross and truly we shall be blessed. Alleluia!

HOME

December 12 – Prayer for Life

Our Lady of Guadalupe, a feast day here in America.

O Patroness of the Unborn, truly spread your arms to protect the innocents from being further slaughtered. Pray for a new spirit to fall upon this country (and world), one which respects life, one which loves life, one which cherishes every newborn child sent by the Father of Life, who is Life itself. May the womb again become a sacred home, all violence having fled from its borders. How we need you to intercede!

How well a Catholic woman from Denmark speaks of the spiritual malaise upon her country, as in most of the West, tracing its source to the practice of contraception and the mentality against life it has terribly encouraged. What hope have we but a miracle like that at Tepeyac nearly 500 years ago.

December 13 – Christmas Tree

Picked up a beautiful Christmas tree. As the worker, who'd said he was pretty good at choosing trees, went to get his scissors to open his selection, Sylvia found another one that looked good. She also noticed the bottom of the tree the worker picked seemed bare. And she was right about both trees.

The tree she picked is so full, all the way to the bottom. One of the best I've ever seen. She said, to me and to the worker, that she had prayed to the Blessed Mother to help us find a tree that would honor her Son... and she did. The tree does make the home at Christmastime.

December 14 – St. John of the Cross

I woke to thunder, and in the still dark morning read in the Office St. John of the Cross' words on the necessity of suffering if one is to find the glory of God. And in the gospel the Son of Man tells of His own suffering, as well as that of John the Baptist.

Though still feeling sick, and though it was raining when I came out of church, I drove alone to Planned Parenthood to take up my place there. And the rain stopped, and I was able to give witness unimpeded.

And another spiritual man who lives in the rooming house across the street admired the Divine NAME around my neck, and we spoke of the Silence of the LORD, that it is His language. Few have spoken better of this Silence than John of the Cross. (And we hear today of Elijah, who was blessed to know the still, small voice of the mighty LORD.)

December 15 – Gaudete Sunday

Joy in the Cross. There *must* be joy in the Cross, or it is not of Christ. This begins to dawn on me more clearly this morning. Then the priest speaks well of the doubt and darkness that are so much a part of the spiritual life, noting Mother Teresa and St. Thérèse (and John of the Cross) and the long trials they underwent, the Cross under which they labored... and the light of Christ that was present within them throughout, their faith not wavering but growing stronger. He quoted Thérèse saying the Lord was so merciful because He chose a time for her suffering when she was able to bear it.

How easily we forget that Christ died on a Cross and it is this same Cross we must carry. And how easy it is to forget that it is this Cross that leads to salvation... and so, what joy it should bring.

December 16 – The Truth

Surprised (pleasantly) to hear our retired priest give such a strong pro-life homily today – *Planned Murder, bodies torn in pieces...* He couldn't help but speak the truth.

Spoke later with an elder member of the parish who mentioned that a priest told him in the old days the dioceses controlled what the priests could say in their homilies re abortion, wanting not to offend anyone, I suppose.

HOME

But the truth will set you free – how true that is! And so we see why our society is so enslaved. But the Word of God cannot be chained, and, indeed, all is in the Lord's hands.

Someday.

December 17 – Entreating

Begging the Lord for increased purity this Advent season, seeking to overcome any vestiges of my past life. I notice (during Stations) that as I recognize my need for virtue, the trials and temptations come; as long as I don't, I am allowed to go on without too much trouble, except for the trouble of the sin itself, which should prove the greatest trouble if we truly seek the Lord.

But I am trying, and as I say, entreating the Lord's grace and favor, at least recognizing the need. Let me not be forgetful but have faith in the power of the Lord to heal me, to continue to desire the attainment of greater virtue. What is more important than the heart?

December 18 – Adoration Chapel

The adoration chapel in NJ has been a bit difficult to coordinate since we've been back in Florida. Of course, we are not there to take hours, but neither is the adorer who is really the foundation, taking the first hour virtually every day. Another major (3-hour) adorer recently had to step back... and more people have just been absent (not to mention those who have moved away).

But though at times it has been unusually trying (ordinarily it mostly runs itself), the Lord has provided. Another person who has been going to the chapel almost every day has been able to fill in well, as have a couple of regular subs and a new family that has been very available. It reminds me it is the Lord's will and His chapel, and He does take care of His own. May He continue to bless this home away from home.

December 2019

December 19 – Away from Home

Working on Sylvia and her sister's tickets to the Philippines for their nephew's wedding in a couple of months. So far to travel to get back home, halfway around the world. Hard for me to imagine what it would be like to live so far from where one is born and raised. At least she has family in the U.S., and there are Filipinos everywhere we go (especially in the Catholic churches)... and she has been here longer than there now, so I suppose that changes one's perspective. But still, I wonder, as I have with my ESL students over the years, how people can move so far away from home, and so often alone. Only God could give me strength for that, since we are all His children and live in His Kingdom ultimately.

December 20 – Books

Working on flyer for books and changes to website, and receiving boxes of books in the mail day after day as I prepare for four or five conferences coming up in the next few months or so. Now that I have switched to a new, and significantly cheaper, means of publishing and printing – including the republishing of a few older titles – I find myself more encouraged to promote their sales. So a rather exciting time for this part of my life. We will see how the Lord blesses this call, this work. I do it all for Him and for His Word to go forth, I pray, through these poor writings, from which I make no profit otherwise.

Since I was a child I have loved books (like Dr. Seuss) and remember getting them in the mail in a flat cardboard box. I still find them and (now) the making of them, and holding them in my hands, rather inspiring. So glad for the few souls who have benefited from them.

December 21 – Memories

Had another dream of my hometown. Started when I called my childhood friend in the middle of the night (accidentally) and woke

HOME

him up. He said something about going into NYC, but I told him Christmas is very near and I didn't think I could make it. Then I was walking (at night still) through another part of the city (where I stay when I return now), but soon found myself in my old neighborhood walking along a street a couple of blocks from my childhood house. When I turned a corner heading for my old block... it wasn't there anymore: it was all stores (like the central street is), really like one big mall. Even the style of the buildings was unrecognizable.

I thought, as people often say when their parish church or school closes, or their old house is knocked down: "They've taken my memories." But then I realized – perhaps influenced by a film my wife and I watched the night before (wherein the artist character's theme was that we never really lose our memories) – that they remain with us. This was a thought very much like the one at the heart of my conversion, when I realized that the child I had been, the child we all once were, is *still* inside, is not gone. (Childlike innocence was the one thing I could hold on to while going through this long period of painful purgation leading, thankfully, to rebirth.) I realized the memories are not taken away, only the *reminders*. The memories do remain, always. Though they need to be purged at times and encouraged at others, they are *always* with us.

And what is most important extends beyond childlike innocence or the memories of happy times: what is important is truly the Kingdom of Heaven. May our memory, our intellect, and our will bring us there.

(Today was very blessed. Felt inspired to do the Lord's work, especially after Confession this morning. I was consistently thankful to the Lord as I found His presence very near throughout the day, particularly in clearly answered prayer.)

December 22 – Light through the Darkness

These are the darkest days of the year, and that was emphasized by rain throughout the day. But now the light has begun to increase, starting today. And in three days the Light will come to us. Soon the Christ Child will be born into our midst, into our darkness.

December 2019

Before Mass today we hear from a member of a group that is very successful at helping drug addicts find their life again. He told the story of his own descent into hell, and his being raised up again. And on TV I see a show featuring members of Cenacolo, a blessed Catholic community that also saves the lives of the drug-addicted and others lost in the darkness of this world.

The Light comes through the darkness, piercing it, making it bleed, and bringing new life. As it has for me.

December 23 – Tasks

Two days before Christmas and trying to get things done before the Octave comes.

There are so many tasks with which we must be busied day to day – it is not a simple life we lead in this place and time. Though Sylvia and I do try to live as simply as we can, and simpler than most, still, there is much to do, much to take care of... cooking and cleaning, laundry and shopping, finances and fixing this or that... not to mention volunteer work or writing or teaching. But I try to keep the Lord in all the little tasks that must be accomplished each day, and I think of these as I ready to leave the chapel kneeling before Him in my "face time" at the end of Holy Hour.

Stay with us, Lord.
Let us be near you even when away from your House and prayer.

December 24 – Sacristan

We arrived at the door of the church building this early morning at the same time as two sacristans (each of whom seemed surprised to see the other), one with us unlocking the door from the outside as the other unlocked the door beside it from the inside. No one else around.

Inside the chapel Sylvia went over to help one of the (elderly) sacristans replace the votive candles. As she was over there (and as I prayed the Rosary), a profound reflection came upon me and I

HOME

imagined that in ten or 15 years I would not be here... and perhaps Sylvia would be the sacristan for the parish (as she had been for a couple of churches back in NJ).

I wondered if I would be able to see her from where I was, or pray for her. I thought perhaps not if in Purgatory, where I expect to be (unable to give all my heart to the Lord), though likely so if in Heaven. And I thought I'd better do all I can to be able to watch over her when I've passed on. It should be a goal to guide me.

(This is the chapel in which we were married and where I had an inner sense we would return and find a home well before moving to Florida.)

December 25 – Cloudy Christmas

Woke to a cloudy, somber day, which only reflected my outlook. How can one be joyful, even on Christmas, thinking of one friend whose daughter is suffering so much from depression that he is afraid she will end up in the ER again, and another friend who has been sleeping five days now... and then listening to the Holy Father (in his Urbi et Orbi address) repeatedly offering prayers for places experiencing war and poverty and persecution, as well as reading of these places in my newspaper. Then the first person I meet at church tells me his dad is now in a nursing home and his caretaker brother is sick. Perhaps worst of all is thoughts of friends and family who have been away from the Church for years, if not decades... and then becoming very conscious that more than half of the people going up for Communion do not know or believe in the Real Presence, and so may be eating unto their condemnation (with my wife serving as an extraordinary minister to them). As I sit in mourning, the Lord (and Our Lady) seems to say: "Now you know how your sin makes me feel." And there is indeed no greater weight than my own sins.

How I need the Lord to bring light to the darkness of this world and my soul. For this should not be a day for tears but joy. My hope now is set on the fact that Christmas Day lasts eight days, and so there is time for the Spirit of peace to fill me, even in the darkness.

(And now I read Our Lady's message speaking of souls "heading towards spiritual death" and the waning peace on earth. Only vision of Heaven can help us through.)

December 26 – St. Stephen

Day 2 of the Christmas Octave. Another story of a suffering teen (severe mouth cancer), the granddaughter of a friend of a friend.

The priest points out well the significance of this feast of the first martyr following immediately upon the great feast of the birth of our Savior: for the Cross He was born. And a friend tells me of a saint who was told by the Lord that the Cross was with Him from the moment He was conceived. I have long been aware that being born into this world was a Cross for Jesus, though it brings us the greatest joy.

Now we suffer with Him in this world of darkness, hoping to bring to it a ray of light. And so my friend takes food to the poor as I remain at the entrance of Planned Parenthood. And the stories of his prison ministry make us both say, there but for the grace of God go I.

December 27 – Purgatorial Dream

Dream of my father. Had drawn a clearer portrait of himself (than the one in our garage). Then in the cellar back in our Jersey City home, a rather large, collage-type narrative painting. The principal scene I recall was of him in a hospital bed, suffering. He said, "Whenever I move, I am in pain." He died suddenly so this was not a recounting of his life but seemed something he might be undergoing in Purgatory. A very purgatorial dream calling for greater prayer for his soul.

St. John, great mystic and writer, pray for us,
that we too might draw close to Christ.

December 28 – Holy Innocents

Rather ironic that it is not until this martyrs' feast on the fourth day of the Octave that I begin to sense the joy and peace of Christmas, perhaps aided by repeated mention of joy in the Liturgy of the Hours, and certainly by my Confession. I realize that however great the misery of the world and the mourning it brings to the Christian soul, the arms of the Lord are much wider and able to embrace it all and turn it to joy.

Today we celebrate those infant martyrs slaughtered by the rage of Herod against the Christ Child. And I remember the slaughter of the innocents at the founding of the nation of Israel, when Pharaoh in his fear of their growing numbers ordered all the Hebrew boys drowned. But baby Moses was drawn from the water to lead the Israelites up out of slavery to the Promised Land. And can we hope that the blood of the innocents killed in the womb today will also serve by the grace and power of God as seed for the flourishing of the Church?

Though we had just been there two days ago (on the feast of St. Stephen), since it is the feast of the Holy Innocents, my wife and I return to Planned Parenthood, where so much innocent blood has been shed. What can we do but witness to life?

December 29 – Holy Family

Always disappointed when I see the option to cut out (in short form) the "Wives, be submissive to your husbands.... Husbands, love your wives" passage from Paul's letter. There is no question that there is a major problem (perhaps *the* major problem) in the Church and in the world regarding the essential relationship of man and woman, husband and wife. But instead of addressing it, it is ignored. Healing will never come without true teaching on the nature of marriage.

But (praise God) my fears are not realized today, since the lector read the controversial paragraph. And as she did, it seemed there was a hush over the congregation, a silence of listening ears, ears appreciative of being nourished with the truth of the Gospel, of the Word of God regarding marriage and family.

We are thirsting for this truth as wayward children thirst for discipline. May Mother Church feed this thirst, I pray, that families today may be holy.

December 30 – To Joy

Nearing the end of the Christmas Octave and my wife and I continue to watch Christmas films on TV most nights. They seem to get better and bring more tears. (But I do cry rather easily.)

The corner into joy was turned yesterday and Christmas has pretty well sunk in. It has been a blessing to be more aware of the Eight Days this year... and to discover better the sorrow that is part of joy, that leads to joy.

Let your love be founded on the rock that is Christ,
who suffers to bring joy.

December 31 – Eight Days

I explain to family at New Year's Eve dinner that Christmas *begins* (not ends) on December 25, that for eight days it is still Christmas Day and the season continues another week or two.... So few people know or recognize this, even in the Church, so greatly influenced by the consumerist culture (which begins the Christmas season in November, if not October) that it is nearly impossible to get the Church calendar known – even if they may be aware of the 12 days of Christmas somewhere in the back of their minds.

But for me this year it has become very real; I have been very aware of these eight days of Christmas. And today a call to purity is upon my soul, a special Christmas blessing. What more could we ask from the Christ Child than the purity of heart that enables us to see God?

HOME

January 1, 2020 – The Spirit Moves

On this Octave Day I cannot but wish everyone a Merry Christmas, for it is the fulfillment of the feast. And I find myself blessed in going from one thing to another in a series of continuous movements, I pray, in the Spirit. Though the actions were all rather mundane – organizing boxes of books recently received, reading a religious magazine, walking with my wife, shaving, praying, eating, TV... still, it reminded me of my sense of how the Spirit moved in the novice house of the Friars of the Renewal, especially in one of my visits there. Someone would ring the bell asking for food, an incident would occur outside the house, and the friar I was visiting would go to address the need immediately. I saw that it was indeed the Spirit that moved the friars, that organized their day, and how open they were to His inspiration. This sense was particularly noticeable today in the way that no sooner would I complete one activity then the next would present itself... and I would be off to take care of it. It was as if the Spirit were organizing my day without my knowing.

May the Spirit organize all our days, this year and always.
Mama Mary, pray for us.

January 2 – Living in a Miracle

Praying the Lord order all my days; it is wonderful to see, to know, His hand at work, to see how the day is ordered by Him, to live in His will, His miracle. May all days and all things of each day be ordered by Him. This is living in a miracle. This is being productive, being fruitful. In this way we become flesh of His flesh. May every hour be His.

January 3 – Pure Heart

Purity. What is it and how is it found? It is in the heart, this much is clear. It is and must be at the heart of our being. But that only tells us where it is, not what it is or how it may be found.

It must *be* the heart, the very life of us. And what is true life but God Himself? And so, what must we be but of God, His children, one with Him?

Purity is found in union with the Lord and with His will. And so we must live in His will, be subject to His call. But who has ears to hear the call of the Lord? How can we be so holy as ever to have ears open to obey the Lord, we who are so deaf? And if not deaf, distracted, blinded by so many things.

Purity is found apart from all things, for it is found in God, who is holy, set apart from all things.

O Lord, purify my heart. Set me apart from all sin and all attachment to sin, from all things of the flesh, the world, and the devil, that I might live with you, who are Life itself. Lead me on right paths with you, for I can see very little of the way to perfection. Clear the path before me.

January 4 – Still at the Gates

Dark clouds gather over Planned Parenthood today, and the only client inside has a Choose Life plate. Is there an ominous end on the horizon for this place of death... and can light be brought within it? I can only stand and pray in silence, still at the gates, putting all in God's hands.

And that same silence and stillness is upon me as I kneel before Our Lady and the Tabernacle praying the Luminous Mysteries after my Confession this morning. All we can do, the best we can do, is submit ourselves to the LORD's holy will, as St. Elizabeth Seton preached to her sisters.

January 5 – The Real Presence

Anniversary of my dad's death. Were planning a trip to an outdoor historic site on this Sunday of pleasant weather... but, somewhat miraculously, my depressed friend who I am only occasionally able to bring Communion (since he sleeps most of the time and is

HOME

usually only awake at night) was available when I called today. That put us behind schedule a half hour or more, and we felt a little rushed, so put off our day out.

I had earlier promised Our Lady if we weren't able to go out today, I would write letters to the editor I had been considering (one later published)... and I eventually accomplished that task, though not without hesitation.

I continue to be amazed that, though lack of belief in the Real Presence is so widespread and so well known (another alarming poll recently), nothing is said as everyone in the church walks up to receive the Lord. (And what of the ignorance of various other obvious, serious problems, like missing Mass regularly, practicing contraception, viewing pornography... all by large numbers?)

It is so obvious, it is unbelievable that nothing is done when the most essential tenet of the Faith is so greatly abused. So many approach the altar without discerning the Lord's Body... and *nothing is said.*

January 6 - He Is Here

Day of Epiphany (though celebrated yesterday here in the U.S.). The Lord manifests Himself in so many ways, if we only had our eyes and mind open to see Him. In all things He can be seen, but our vision is elsewhere, distracted by what is before us, and so, unable to look into the depths, into the heart of things, where God is.

We go from one thing to another so often breathless. Be still before the Lord, before His Hand at work. This is not your world - you are not the Creator and Sustainer of Life. He Is.

Let His Light dawn upon your mind and heart,
and your soul breathe as one with Him.
He is here.

January 2020

January 7 – Heartbreaking Work

Three-plus hours at Planned Parenthood. So many incidents. Had to counsel more than usual on a Tuesday since a few people were home sick.

It really is heartbreaking work (which is why I tend to let others do it on abortion days). Two Hispanic women went in, one with a little girl. The abortion-minded one surprised me by saying to leave her alone, but her friend came back out soon after and she was open to life – had a child at 14. Spoke with her a while and asked her to call her friend (they wouldn't let her in with a child) to tell her to request to see her ultrasound.... She did, but her friend did not come out. One woman did come out in tears, though, saying she decided not to have an abortion.

The good stories are a blessing, but there is so much bad news, so much death here. It is not easy to keep from tears.

January 8 – Joyful News

I hear (in tears) from another counselor this evening that the Hispanic woman *did* come out after I left, and drove away! And the counselor tells me of another turnaround, due to her selflessness and that of another witness to life who stayed at PP to the bitter end. So there were three turnarounds yesterday! What joy this fills me with. I can't help but cry.

Thank you, Lord, for your blessings this day.
O let the whole society become pro-life, we pray!
Then all will know this joy.

January 9 – His Light at Work

Praying to be a child of light, offering myself up to the Lord for the good of those around me, those with whom I come in contact, I realize how unconscious I am of any good I might do; it is the Lord's doing, it is the Lord's blessing, His light in me.

And we must give ourselves to that light, for the love of God and others, and indeed become children of light.

It is almost frightening to think how the Lord might work through us, and how united we can be to Him. This is the work of grace.

January 10 – Your Will Be Done

John says today he is writing to let us know we have eternal life. That is the same light of which we are so often unaware: the eternal life of the Spirit within us by Baptism and strengthened by Holy Communion. May John's purpose be accomplished and we become aware of what we do not know.

The priest in his homily today speaks beautifully of how our prayer must always be for the Lord's will to be done, even in the most difficult circumstances and amidst the greatest suffering. (Gave example of his friend dying in the hospital.) Practicing this immediately toward all the intentions I hold for desperate situations brought a very blessed sense of peace and joy: freedom is found in this truth.

But it was put to the test when I found out upon returning home that the troubled daughter of an acquaintance, for whom I have been praying, has not been doing well this Christmas Season but is in therapeutic care every day.

May your will be done, O Lord,
for truly you love us more than we can love.

January 11 – YHWH

For my penance the priest asked me to think about John the Baptist's words: "He must increase; I must decrease." And as I did so, I realized this is best done by speaking the (silent) NAME of God, for then we give ourselves over to the Lord completely, entering into His Presence and, so, forgetting our own cares and concerns, our own life, our own pride.

During Mass I had experienced a quiet moment of contemplation when, after the priest led the congregation in a time of personal holy communion, I realized how words can distract from such communion... and as I entered the Silence, spoke the NAME (YHWH), in an instant I was deep in prayer, so deep I remained kneeling a few seconds after all had risen for the final prayer. I could have, and would have liked to have, continued kneeling in that silence a long time, but was conscious enough to realize how that would stand out.

I really must practice this great gift the Lord has given me and make it the focus of my prayer life, of my life. I must stop being discouraged because no one joins me and there is no movement toward any kind of order. This should not keep me from practicing such grace myself. In this I should find my principal home.

January 12 – Wombal Memories

Spoke of my wombal memories to my wife and to my troubled friend, whom we brought Communion. Don't usually open up like that, but the topic of memory came up and at Mass I had been remembering the mobile over my crib and other early memories, like the shade and light of the edges of curtains.

I do have clear memories of infancy. One photo shows me potty training when a little over a year old. I recall well my parents pushing the door open to take the photo and my embarrassment as I reached to close the door. The only specific wombal memory I have is of my father's voice, I believe during my mom's long labor. But of the womb I sense, or have sensed, my body like a stone balloon, as if I were wrapped in gauze... and I hear a heartbeat surrounding me. It is very peaceful and I need to get into a very relaxed, meditative state to remember it. (Most of this intense contemplation leading to discovery of early memories occurred during my conversion period, at the age of twenty-three or so.)

I suppose this was my original home. (And I seemed not to want to leave it, considering the eventual need for a Caesarean.)

January 13 - Following Jesus

First day of Ordinary Time and Peter and Andrew, James and John, leave all behind to follow the Lord. And the priest speaks of fulfilling our potential, becoming fully human... being disciples of Christ.

I think initially of my writings, which I would tend to do anyway, but the thought was particularly spurred because this is the priest who once encouraged me to give talks, something I haven't done. This may indeed be a way I could better bear fruit, but I realize too that the call to fullness in Christ is primarily an interior one - conforming our hearts to His.

And the question is begged: have I left all to follow Jesus? Do I? I orient my day and my activities, prayers, etc. around Him and His work... but certainly greater zeal could be found.

All that I am, O Lord, I give to you this day.
I pray I follow where you lead.

January 14 - The Lost Sheep

Another day of blessed pro-life witness at Planned Parenthood - three saves and greater openness to the call of life. One woman has been present at most of the six saves in the last two weeks and spent close to six hours witnessing each week.

I can't help but think how painful this must be for her. She watched about ten clients pass her by and enter for abortions before one turned around. Then two more turned around, and this is a great joy. But the pain is like Christ on the Cross to stand in this place of death and feel your heart break for those who do *not* turn around.

Jesus leaves the ninety-nine to find the one lost soul because each soul means so much to Him. And those who imitate our Lord can't help but suffer to watch the loss of life, and the loss of souls.

January 2020

May they find their way home, we pray;
may they find their way home.

(And today there did seem greater receptivity generally, more eye contact and genuine exchanges. We are all humans and so should care for one another as brothers.)

January 15 – Leaning Towards Death

Assisted suicide film is on in the background as I write this. How life is devalued; how crass man can become.

It seems to me the cause of all this leaning towards death is a lack of love, and especially the love of family. Of course, a turning from the love of God is the most essential cause, but looking at the circumstances of the world, we see people who are lonely, who do not have families, have not known the joy of a blessed childhood in a loving family... and so they cannot understand why people would want to live (or should live) beyond their usefulness – just being with a person, just *loving a person*, is not enough, is something they cannot grasp.

Love cannot be grasped; like life, it must be lived. We must bring love to society to return its hope or there will be only darkness on the horizon.

January 16 – Spiritual State

As I was leaving adoration and kneeling the final time near the door, I felt myself quite overwhelmed, entering into the spiritual dimension, as if in another world, where the body, the physical universe, does not take precedence, is not reality, but reality is the Spirit. Again I would have stayed a long time and perhaps gotten lost in that blessed sense... but I rose up as my wife exited the doors.

Maybe sometime I will just remain in that state. Someday I pray it will be my home.

January 17 – One of Those Days

One of those days when everything seems to go wrong: badly stubbed my toe, bent pipe trying (unsuccessfully) to fix leaking shower, bought wrong shower bar, ants on kitchen table (which remain even after spraying).... Makes me think I really don't want to own a home.

But we must praise God for the problems that help to purify us of attachments; we know that suffering leads to joy. And I'm sure all will be fixed, all will be well, even here in this earthly home.

January 18 – Resilience

Spent a couple of hours shopping online for a new kitchen set, without a decision; waiting till Monday for plumber to fix shower faucet; but big toe seems to be healing up.

Things sometimes take time, especially things that matter. But the suffering – and I think of Haiti, about which I have been reading, particularly regarding the earthquake ten years ago – often leads to a blessed joy. It is as if the suffering causes the joy as we conquer that which we thought had conquered us, as we realize the power of God at work in our lives.

Some things are hard, arduous, but patience and resilience indeed conquers all, by God's grace (especially in relationships).

January 19 – Becoming Married

I feel of late as if I am becoming married to my wife, which I suppose is strange to say after nearly fifteen years of marriage. But I see a greater cooperation and a greater love, a greater intimacy growing. I have said that Sylvia is my home in this world, and that seems to be becoming a reality.

I think having lived mostly as a monk for so long, there was a certain hesitancy in me (maybe in both of us) to accept married life. This had been told to me by at least one spiritual director, who instructed me to overcome that obstacle... but it seems only now I am realizing the problem and coming to accept the state in which the Lord has placed me, placed us.

Mother Mary, pray for us whose marriage is consecrated to Jesus through you.

January 20 – God's Time

Plumber was expected so couldn't make usual Mass. Had planned on going out to early Mass, but couldn't wake up, so gave up on the idea and put it in God's hands (always an evening Mass a half hour away).

Then after holding my wife a while, I got up just a few minutes before I usually leave for early Mass... and not tired anymore, and skipping breakfast and exercise, etc., somehow made it there about the same time, able to do all prayers as usual before Mass.

I have often said that when I am late I end up early, and when I am early I end up late, which is one indication of how time is in God's hands, and in our faith in those hands.

January 21 – Stations of Suffering

Praying the Stations this morning was a blessed paradox. I try to pray them when the church is empty as possible, but at the church we visit on Tuesdays (abortion day) one Mass follows another with only a half hour between. Though there are usually only a few people present anyway after the initial Mass, today the bishop was celebrating our annual pro-life Mass (commemorating Roe v. Wade), followed by a Prayer Walk at Planned Parenthood, so the church was getting full.

But, though I was aware of the people around me as I performed the (unfortunately) unusual practice of praying the Stations, and so somewhat self-conscious... at the same time I found great intimacy with the Lord at each station. I found myself more conscious of

HOME

the Lord's suffering as the Stations became more real, as did prayers for plenary indulgence.

This sense of the suffering Christ seemed appropriate for this dreadful anniversary as well as for our weekly witness on this abortion day, a day on which the traffic was tragically heavy. Appropriate also was praying in the windy shade on this particularly cold day (for Florida). Cold connotes death and so suffering, an appropriate offering in this place of death. But we pray for the mercy of the Lord.

January 22 – Mothers

Anniversary of Roe v. Wade. A day of mourning. (Violet day.)

Mothers of two friends have died in the past few days: one of the woman who leads our sidewalk counselors and the other of my Jewish former boss.

And Judaism seems a running theme today: aside from learning of my former boss' loss from my current Jewish supervisor, and communicating with them both by email (the latter also provided contact info for another Jewish supervisor), I also have an email exchange with the Jewish Catholic (convert) scholar who vetted my book on the Jerusalem Bible (O.T.)... with whom I attempted to be humorous by facetiously speaking in a Jewish voice. And a show I watch this evening centers around the Hasidic community in NYC.

There is nothing like a Jewish mother, of course – for Mary is the Mother of all believers – but such blessed motherhood extends to all mothers, who genuinely share in it... or at least should in any decent society. Someday. How I pray.

O Lord, bring new life! Mama Mary, pray for us.

January 23 – Altar Baby

During the Rosary before Mass this morning, I looked over and there was a baby boy crawling energetically down the center aisle toward the altar. His mother chased him down each time, but his crawling to the altar repeated unabated for quite a while. He was eventually able to make it into the sanctuary near the altar since there is just a short step up (in the chapel). It really was the kind of thing about which one cannot help but smile, and seemed especially appropriate at this time of year. A couple of times he just sat up and smiled in front of the altar and it reminded me of some of St. Faustina's visions of the baby Jesus on the altar during consecration.

And at the pro-life Vigil Mass in Washington D.C. (before tomorrow's March for Life), Archbishop Naumann gave an incisive homily about how evil is termed good in our twisted, *Twilight Zone* society.

Pray for the babies! And pray for our country,
that it find its heart again.

January 24 – Media Blind

Up early and out early to Mass so could put together new kitchen set and watch the March for Life and the *hundreds of thousands* that show up to walk up Constitution Avenue like an army of absolute peace and love. And for the first time a president spoke live.

But this largest of human rights demonstrations is routinely ignored by the mainstream media. It is as if we have two countries: the real one where people live and breathe (and march in great numbers), and the one the media invents. But the truth will be revealed in the end, we know.

January 25 – God's Creatures

Standing at my post on the isolated street behind Planned Parenthood, I look at the trees and the birds and the houses... and I see how the animals are made for man. Some are stronger, some are faster, some are so beautiful... but they are all as signs for man to behold, messages from the LORD God showing His presence and His love for us. They are to be admired but not worshipped;

they are to be our servants, but not abused. Man is at the center of the universe in the image of God and His love and glory must be expressed through us His blessed creatures. And so all His creatures should be loved, appreciated for the gift they are from a good God.

January 26 – The Blind and the Dead

A man whom I was giving Communion in the nursing home asked if I was blind, because I tend to close my eyes when I pray. And for the first time in twenty-five years of this service, I encountered a patient who had died. I was directed to his room by mistake (not a Catholic), but when I got there and was told he had died, I prayed over him a moment.

The blind and the dead. It is who we all are. In fact, in the night I woke up wondering if perhaps I was having a stroke. It was likely just some digestive issue, but it was enough for my wife to get out of bed to tend to me for a while.

We never know. Let our eyes be open, open to the coming of the Lord, repentant of our sins.

January 27 – Lack of Commitment

Gathering books into boxes for first conference in a couple of weeks. Had a chance to go to a catechetical conference two days ago but was not able to overcome obstacles.

I wonder about my resolution and willingness to sacrifice, in particular when it comes to my writings. When is reason necessary and when does faith take over? Perhaps I will never get anywhere because of a lack of zeal, of commitment. And I am getting old.

How shall I today be your disciple, Lord?
How will I hear, and heed, your call?
(I am not only blind but deaf.)

January 2020

January 28 – Kind and Gentle

My homeless friend stopped by preaching the Word (as he does so well) while I was at Planned Parenthood holding a sign offering help at the pregnancy clinic next door. He spoke of our need to accept and reflect the Father's love, and when he mentioned the words "kind and gentle," it struck a chord because the priest had used these same words in his recommendation during my last Confession. I teared up with the truth as we spoke about it. ("Love is patient, love is kind…")

Sometimes we just don't see our sins as God does and so must pray to have our eyes opened to our selfishness.

January 29 – The Change

Coordinating sidewalk counselor training with the national group we joined a few years ago. Not for over a month, but settling the participants at this time and getting pretty good response.

More and more people are stepping forward, especially since the *Unplanned* movie last year (which we will be showing in the parish again in a month, just as 40 Days for Life (and Lent) kicks into gear). The tide does seem to be turning, but the powers that be in this culture of death are not easily overcome… except perhaps by prayer, and in the mercy of God.

There is such a disconnect in this country between the cultural elites, who are small in number but, as I say, a powerful minority controlling media, entertainment, education, etc.… and the people, who are ridiculed by them.

Slowly we awaken, though, to the truth.
(And one day the change will seem quite sudden, and complete.)

January 30 – Coming to Pass

Sylvia has been asked to serve as sacristan one day a week: I watch the vision I had Christmas Eve come to pass. I was the first to hear the request (via email). And because of some minor ailments, and receiving yearly life insurance statement, have thought more of my own mortality in recent days. So, yes, perhaps the vision will come to pass, sooner or later – can't say I have been preparing particularly well, though some movement has been made re care of my wife.

January 31 – Frugality

A certain cheapness comes through today. I tend to be overly frugal. Frugality was very necessary when I lived in virtual poverty for years, and it served me well and provided good skills in "learning how to do without." But this talent for saving money can become an overconcentration on not wanting to waste anything, and so lead to a lack of generosity. I can be like the Pharisees who tithe but whose almsgiving, and especially regular (and extraordinary) expenditures, become constricted by a selfishness, or at least a fear of not saving all that is possible. Old habits are hard to break, even when they are not so needed anymore.

But at Mass this morning I offer all I have to the Lord in the most sincere prayer I can muster. May He give me a generous heart.

February 1 – Grace of Repentance

While witnessing (in the rain) at Planned Parenthood, was witnessed to by two homeless men – my preacher friend and a man they call "the pastor." With the pastor I spoke of David and his sin, but most of all of his repentance, his readiness to turn to the Lord (something the priest emphasized in his homily this morning). And I realized: it is not the size of our sin that matters but the depth of our repentance. One could sin greatly (as did Paul, too), but if he returns to the Lord with a contrite heart, he will be reconciled to Him, back in His grace, and in a better place than someone who sins only little but refuses to recognize his fault, hardening his heart. Refusing to repent of even the smallest sin can keep us from the Lord and His grace.

And my preacher friend stopped to tell us of what the Lord taught him today: that what He has begun in us, He will complete - and especially that it is *He* who brings it to fruition, not us.

Amen. Do your work in me, Lord.

February 2 - Smile

Presentation of the Lord (Sunday).

Felt myself shining like a child of light on this blessed feast day. Not sure where the smile came from, except the Lord.

I remember looking up the word "smile" years ago, tracing its etymology, and finding that it has a common root with the word "miracle." And that makes a lot of sense. For in the smile, the true smile, is the light of Christ, and so His presence... and so it is indeed miraculous.

O Lord, let us shine your light, always. Let us live in your miracle. ("My light shines from within," I hear now from the next room.)

February 3 - Prayer in Disaster

Weeping and wailing we come to you, dear Lord, praying for those we love, those who are sick or those who have died... and how do we get our prayer answered except that we have faith?

Day after day more intentions come to us, more and more people seeking the healing of the Lord, physically, emotionally, spiritually. And so, on this feast of St. Blaise may our prayers be answered through his intercession. May your will be done in all things, Lord, even in the disasters that befall us.

HOME

As I write the news is ablaze with stories of a virus sweeping through China and increasingly other parts of the world. It has put my wife's trip to the Philippines in jeopardy as no one is currently being admitted there from Hong Kong, her transfer point.

Does the Lord bring such scourges to places like China and Australia (where terrible fires have been raging) to bring them to repentance? It may be. But we should all remember we are all in need of repentance or we will all likewise come to catastrophic ends.

February 4 – Peter

Was inspired today to respond to an email from a devout Christian friend with exhortation regarding the primacy of Peter and the need for a Magisterium. He is a former Methodist who was writing about the recent split in that church over the teaching on homosexuality, and who proclaimed the importance of following the Word of God, for him, the Bible alone.

I mentioned the first Council at Jerusalem and how Peter silenced the cacophony of voices by standing up and declaring that we are saved by grace – without his word they would still be arguing among themselves, as the hundreds, if not thousands, of churches do today.

The Church is our Mother, a gift from the Lord for our teaching and nourishment along the way to Heaven. We ignore Her at our own peril.

February 5 – Beloved

As the gospel was read I had a particular insight regarding Jesus' saying a prophet is not honored "in his own house," seeing the "house" as the individual himself, that is, a person's inability to recognize the glory of God in himself. I had been thinking about how poorly I may be using the Lord's gifts because of a kind of low self-esteem or lack of appreciation of them, and how I might better employ them (giving talks?).

Then the priest in his homily immediately made the same point I just conceived – that the people had a lack of faith in their own dignity as beloved children of God and so could not recognize the divinity of Jesus. And he went on to speak of how important it is to know in the first place our identity as God's beloved... really reading my heart.

I think this may be a significant problem in me, this lack of understanding or awareness of who I am, that *God loves me*, that I may be putting myself down, so to speak.

And perhaps the priest's point that as long as we put ourselves down (not in genuine humility but in a kind of doubt or fear) and fail to recognize we are God's beloved children, we will never find our home, our eternal home in union with the Lord.

And now I recall that as the speaker at the Luncheon preceding Mass recounted how he held a troubled teen and told her just about what we have said above – that she is a beloved child of God – I had tears in my eyes, and they were not just for the girl. We must accept God's love!

February 6 – Worldly Blessings

Been very blessed lately regarding material, worldly things: quick resolve of Sylvia's travel problems (refund), sale of her lot (finally), summer class offer, all replacement books fine (very rare), taxes done today.... For all these things I thank the Lord and find Him watching over me. I suppose my only prayer is that spiritual matters go as well; though I should be grateful, I must not focus on the worldly blessings to the detriment of what matters most.

It is curious that just as I make a sincere prayer to give all things – financial, etc. – to the Lord, He blesses me with these things. But I have checked myself and seem to be continuing to give all to Him. Praise God. All must lead to Heaven.

February 7 – A Pastor's Funeral

Funeral for former long-time pastor of current parish; church packed with a thousand people (SRO). It was a funeral as I have never experienced, both in the numbers and in the sincerity of the attendees, all who had a real love for their priest, as he had for us.

The homily was beautiful, the singing of his signature Irish blessing very poignant (both bringing tears)... but there was nothing to match the outpouring of emotion I felt upon hearing this whole church singing "How Great Thou Art" as a prayer rising up from one heart in intercession for the deceased. I was particularly moved when we sang the chorus the final time: the joy of his being taken home and falling down "in humble adoration" of our one Lord was overwhelming. I had a vision of Father smiling at the gates of Paradise with Jesus as they listened down at our song. How could the Lord resist such a powerful prayer for a poor soul?

February 8 – Hands and Feet

Driving to the men's conference (to sell books) listening to Matt Maher sing about being Jesus' "hands and feet" by feeding the hungry, helping the homeless... I can't help but wonder how well I am serving as a disciple of Christ. Certainly the Church as a whole is His hands and feet, and I do considerable work for pro-life causes, trying to help women in difficult situations make a decision for life. I also sponsor a child overseas, and often speak with the homeless while at Planned Parenthood... but, still, I can't help but wonder if I shouldn't be more so in the trenches, serving more directly and completely. I still remember fondly (decades ago) coordinating a weekly soup kitchen in my parish, and so working and being amongst the homeless on a regular basis. Must keep this in prayer.

Lord, let me truly be your hands and feet.
Let me be open to your will for my life,
wherever it leads.

February 9 – A Call

The Lord was unmistakably speaking to me through His Word today. The first words in the readings were to feed the hungry and help the homeless; the psalm extolled the generous heart... and the gospel called us to be salt and light.

I begged the Lord for a heart for the poor and I realized that means a heart open to everyone – the hungry and the homeless in the streets, my family, and everyone I meet because everyone must be fed: all are hungry.

This doesn't rule out a more particular call to help the obviously poor... and it should not be an excuse for complacency settling in, as I rest up after a busy week and eat too much. But straight from Mass we did go to the nursing homes to bring Communion to the sick, so I guess we were feeding the hungry and caring for those in need.

I was exhausted at Mass when I received this word, and I think that sense contributed to my becoming vulnerable enough to see the poverty in all people. And it made me ready even for death as I began to think more of others (including my wife) than myself.

It should be noted that the priest thoroughly confirmed this call as he exhorted us throughout his homily to care for the poor, using Mother Cabrini as an example, she who founded 67 houses (something a long-time nursing home resident, and eventual friend, to whom I brought Communion reminded me of repeatedly over the years).

Open my heart to your call, O Lord,
to feed the poor, whoever they are and wherever I am.

February 10 – The Poor

The Office of Readings features Paul speaking (in Galatians) about "being mindful of the poor," the very quote I had been considering the past couple of days. And so, further confirmation of the need to be conscious of and helpful toward the poor.

HOME

Here Paul is rather certainly speaking of those lacking the material wherewithal to take care of themselves, and so, though we must be fed with the Word of God as well as bread, and the poorest can be seen as the child in the womb or the souls in Purgatory (for whom I pray daily), the call to help those without cannot be set aside, comes into focus.

And so the call repeating itself is particularly to do more for the hungry and the homeless. I pray that I seek the way the Lord may be leading me, and not become complacent.

February 11 – Jesus Hat

Forgot to mention a dream I had the other night (the first time this call re the poor was repeated) of a troubled boy whom I tried to work with, to love, to show he was loved. He was a real street kid in a threatening environment. Thought of Don Bosco and his work with troubled boys. But I don't think that is the particular call.

Today I try to think of the poor, to pray for and remember them, and as I arrive at Planned Parenthood I say hello to a homeless man, who asks for a dollar. I give it to him happily. And then as we were praying, a homeless woman came by and asked a couple of others for a Jesus hat. I remembered I had one in my car (a distance away) and broke from prayer a moment to ask if she could come back in a little while so I could finish my prayers.... She didn't return – I should have known that and gone to my car right away. But I did get the hat and left it with others who were still present when we left, should she come back.

February 12 – The Sick

Wife had a preventative procedure done today; we thank the Lord that all checked out well. She had to prepare for it with fasting, so it was like having a patient in the house for a couple of days. It's a good thing to care for the sick, especially family, no matter how it might disrupt our schedule.

Somewhat less focused on depressed friend, who called while we were watching television. Gave him maybe three-quarters of my attention, though he may have needed it more so.

February 13 – The Dying and the Desperate

Fellow parishioner dying of cancer sat in front of us today. I told her our depressed mutual friend had told me last night to wish her well the next time I saw her. She said she would pray for him, and after the Mass told me she had offered it up for him.

The dying pray for the desperate. I'm sure the Lord hears these prayers clearly.

February 14 – Wise Evangelization

Priest called us to wise evangelization today. Evangelization, yes; being salt, yes... but as when there is too little salt, food is bland, when there is an overabundance of salt, one wants to spit out the food. So, though he repeatedly encouraged evangelization, and even overt, explicit evangelization when appropriate, his exhortation to be wise and not overdo it was very insightful. And it answered questions on my own mind.

I had been praying about being an image of Christ, His hands and feet, and about Paul's line that "it is no longer I who live but Christ who lives in me," and realizing how far I am from that goal. But perhaps in some more subtle ways I do follow our Lord and His way. May it be so.

February 15 – Open Ears

In Confession after Mass this morning the question of helping the poor came up, and I was already into the conversation before realizing I was speaking to the priest whose homily earlier in the week so reflected my thoughts, and whom I had considered seeking out about the matter.

We realized together that there are all kinds of calls, and he asked me to be open to the Holy Spirit's direction, to the voice of God that is always speaking to us. His guidance is not lacking to those with open ears.

And the members of the St. Vincent de Paul Society were all in attendance at Mass, their annual meeting following. I saluted several of them as they left the chapel (quite a line). I realized I could not join them because after Confession I would soon be going to Planned Parenthood to witness there.

And at PP, where I was particularly joyful and open to the Spirit, I had several conversations with both homeless persons and residents of the rooming house across the street. The Lord does lead us where we should be; let us stay open to His call.

February 16 – Troubles

Thinking of death and dying of late, perhaps because of what is probably a problem with my stomach but sometimes seems to affect my heart, which I have been told is susceptible to a condition termed "the widow maker." Rose in the night in a bit of a sweat and short of breath, weakness in my arms and my heart in my throat. Took about a half hour to get under control, and fall back to sleep. Thought I might have to go to the ER. Made it to Mass but was very weak and a little dizzy.

Trying to get affairs in order; still do not have a will or anything. And hoping not to leave my wife with troubles regarding financial matters, which I watch over, though not in a very organized manner.

At one point today, considering everything and how concerns were piling up and creating anxiety – likely a principal cause of my illness – I took my wife's hand and said, "Come on, let's go to Heaven," as I moved to pull her along. (For a moment I believed it possible.)

February 17 – House

We've been living here in my mother's house for over eight years. She will be 92 soon. For the first time, today Sylvia and I considered buying the house from my mom (essentially, half of it from my brother, since it is to be a co-inheritance). That would, of course, make us more permanently settled in Florida, likely becoming our final home. It is a little scary since I have never owned a house before and am not sure I would like to remain here the rest of my life, though Sarasota has been my second home since I was a child.

We have an appointment with a lawyer in a few days to discuss options.

February 18 – Someday

Learned today that our car, which is under another recall, can be housed in our garage rather than on site (in the sun) at the dealership miles away. Another blessing from the Lord. Though I have experienced a significant amount of stress lately from all the demands upon me, at the same time the Lord has provided remarkable blessings, including a flurry of fruitful activity at Planned Parenthood today, as prayers are offered (by larger numbers), brochures and flowers are given away (with hopes of changing hearts), and at least one couple leaves the death mill to go to the pregnancy clinic next door.

There was a moment, at the time the couple walked out (through the parking lot) that I imagined couple after couple walking out, all realizing at once the terrible reality of what they were doing in taking innocent life.

Someday the truth will cut through all the lies and deception and ignorance, and souls will be enlightened en masse. Then we shall live in a culture of *life*.

February 19 – Sacristan

Watching prophecy play out before me, one which speaks of my own death, but blessings, I pray, upon my wife. Her first day of training as sacristan and reception of the keys to the sacristy.

She is holy and will be holy when I'm gone. She treasures service of the Church and does so reverently and humbly. I am not sad to talk of her serving in this chapel when I am dead and buried, and I am not so frightened of being dead and buried in consideration of her blessed life. There is a peace that comes with sacrifice for the ones we love, wishing only their best.

February 20 – Trust

Trip to lawyer today to set up a trust for my mom (mainly for the house), along with several other things. Looks like we will put off buying the house – the trust seems to avoid later complications well enough.

Prayed to Our Lady and especially St. Joseph before going to the lawyer and, apart from my unnecessarily suspicious attitude, it went very well. St. Joseph has been becoming more real to me, closer to me, of late, principally because we have been doing the recently-published consecration to him. I never felt I knew him before, but the consecration is drawing him up next to Our Lady.

February 21 – Black Car

Since our car is once more under recall, had to get a rental replacement to drive in the meantime. (Should be months again.) Given a black one, the color I would least choose, and not only because it is foolish to drive a dark car in South Florida. But perhaps there is meaning in it, another sign of death... or at least beginning readiness for it as I approach 60 and so enter the stage of senior citizen.

Sylvia also signed the papers for sale of a lot she has held for over thirty years. Very preoccupied with worldly matters of late. But seem to be getting ducks in a row, which was a goal of this time.

February 22 – Helpmate

Sold fifty-one books at women's conference, aided for the first time in a real way by my wife. We worked together well behind the table, she taking an active role. Usually she is more off to partake of the speakers, etc., and generally she has not had much interest in helping me with my writing vocation. So this was a bigger blessing than the books sold, and probably went a long way to create that blessing.

We are planning to attend and get a table at another conference in a few weeks. Another sign of blessing for our marriage.

February 23 – Beloved

In prayer in the chapel before Mass I looked up at Jesus on the Cross and imagined myself reaching out and embracing Him, and so becoming flesh of His flesh, one with Him and His sacrifice of love. In this was great freedom, and great joy. The movement was sparked by a sincere sense of humility, knowing deeply that all I have and all I do of any worth comes from Him as a gift, bestowed from His throne upon the Cross.

Meditation on the love of God was upon my soul yesterday, too, in prayer during adoration at the conference. I learned later that at the time I was sensing deeply that God loves me and loves everyone, the speaker was proclaiming how we are all beloved by the Lord.

February 24 – Readiness

The Lord does seem to be blessing us financially of late, and I seem to have a certain knack for conserving money. I can only hope and pray that the Lord guides me well in utilization of the

HOME

funds He provides. I must not be like Solomon, who made the gathering of wealth an end in itself (and so ended the life of his soul). I must see it as a talent the Lord has entrusted to me to employ wisely and for the good of others.

I have felt a certain peace of late as I work to get affairs in order. It has brought a readiness for death, knowing that others are taken care of and I can leave them with a clear conscience. Yesterday at dinner with my brother I was able to speak (and joke) about death without fear. I don't remember ever feeling such freedom in realizing "we all have to go sometime." This is the best blessing from the Lord.

February 25 – Concerns

Our Lady's message speaks of being "flooded by earthly concerns," and that has certainly been my life in recent weeks... and today is no different as I try to deal with my mom's stocks. I pray I am keeping my head above water. (Into your hands, Lord.) And that sense of freedom remains, despite some impatient driving still.

But our principal concern this day is for the unborn, as we spend a few hours at Planned Parenthood dealing with various situations, including a couple of turnarounds and what seemed a sex trafficker bringing in a girl. The police came, but said there was little they could do, so I appealed to the manager of PP, with whom we have been civil over the years. He seemed sincere as he told me he would check on the matter.

Save us, Lord; look upon our prayers and work –
let us be your hands and feet.

February 26 – Ash Wednesday

A very sad day. Perhaps not for a reason one might think, this being such a major day of penance and fasting. The sadness comes from again having it become painfully clear how poor is the catechesis of the Church, as more than on any other day (though the problem exists on any given day) the church is filled with people who have not been to Mass for many weeks (months, years...), who know not where they are yet come en masse to receive our Lord Jesus Christ in the Sacrament, without a word of caution from the priest.

On it goes. On and on. People don't believe in the Real Presence, they don't attend Mass regularly, they participate in abortion and contraception and pornography... and receive Communion knowing not what they do. They can't be blamed, for indeed they are like sheep without a shepherd. But on it goes. The pain is unbearable.

February 27 – Walk Humbly

Signed all paperwork with lawyer today, mostly for my mom – wills, trust, power of attorney.... All this taking care of legal/financial business continues. It is something I had planned to do at this time, and it seems that plan is a call approved by the Lord. Though it takes me away from writing work, it does seem the will of the Lord and teaches me that one can be called to various things, that what matters is to humbly do whatever is ours to do.

February 28 – "Do You Believe?"

Attended funeral Mass of a faith-filled friend. During the homily the priest spoke of Martha's interaction with Jesus at her brother's tomb. Focusing on Jesus' question following His statement that *He* is the resurrection and the life, the priest seemed to look directly at me for a moment as he repeated: "Do you believe this?" And seeing a measure of doubt in my face seemed to cause him to intensify his preaching on this all-important question.

Do we really believe that even though we die, we still live with Him, in Him who is Life itself? There was doubt in my mind, question, lack of full faith in the Lord which overcomes all fear of death. But the pointed questions helped bring me closer to that necessary, glorious faith.

February 29 – Follow Him

The same priest's homily was again inspirational as his exhortation to "walk with the Lord," to follow Him, led me to look up at the crucifix over the altar and again be moved to reach out to embrace Him, as I repeatedly asked that I might walk in His way. And that path indeed leads to the Cross, where alone there is joy, even in the suffering. Here is our blessed home on this earth. Praise God, may we follow in His way.

And this evening I watch *The Passion of St. Bernadette*.

March 1 – Others First

Praying in the chapel before the same crucifix, seeking how I might walk in the way of the Lord, the answer comes (from the Lord and Our Lady) to put others before myself. And this, though it may not seem so, is a painful word for someone who has been self-centered almost since birth. Hopefully decades of trying to live a Christian life has helped, but still this rings out as a painful call, though a welcome one.

The theme of the day is silence in the desert, and I wonder how that can correspond to putting others first, since one is alone in the desert. Then I remembered my first stay at the Bethlehem Hermitage (twenty years ago) and my first night there alone – I could not have felt closer to the people in my life. It is certainly a paradox; perhaps the truth of it lies in what is in the heart, and in the power of prayer and mortification.

March 2 – Fed by the Poor

How the poor are emphasized in the gospel today, Matthew 24. This gospel I read before giving Communion at the home of my hypomanic friend who rarely leaves the house, living with his mother who also suffers from depression. Thus do I feed the poor today.

March 2020

And upon leaving his house and returning to church for Holy Hour, as I begin my prayer I somehow find myself revived... healed of the sickness I bore most of the day. Thus was I visited in my own poverty by my visit to the poor.

March 3 – Straight Lines

During prayer at Planned Parenthood this morning I lifted my head (which I don't often do) to see a man who had brought a woman inside coming back out the front door. He walked past two (female) counselors and across the street directly toward our lead sign holder, whose sign advertises the free services at the pregnancy clinic next door. My eye fixed on the young man and our sign holder, and I knew he would speak with him.

After they spoke a moment, the man headed back inside, determined to bring his girlfriend to the clinic for a free ultrasound. There were complications (like escorts telling the couple not to go to the clinic, that the ultrasound was not free... causing them to go back inside again), and at one point the man even drove away alone; but the woman eventually came out with her sonogram, convicted not to go through with the abortion.

Later I found myself walking directly toward our lead sign holder with a big smile on my face to tell him the news. As I approached he pointed to a large white bird coming in a straight line behind me toward him. I looked up and saw it fly over us both.

The Holy Spirit was at work today.

March 4 – Vision of YHWH

At the talk before the Luncheon for Life, the priest drew on the board five concentric circles, each representing the most important part of the previous, from "Bible" to "New Testament" to "Gospels" to "Sermon on the Mount" to "Our Father." This not only made perfect sense but led immediately to realization of what is at the very center: the Father Himself, and most particularly His NAME – YHWH – as well as clear, logical explanation of what I understood after my first reading of the Bible cover to cover: it is all *one Word*. And that Word is "YHWH". It was quite an astounding and encouraging revelation.

And it provided not only a kind of proof that the Divine NAME is at the very heart of the Bible, but that the Silence it expresses is at the heart of all words, and at the heart of all Creation. And this led to a vision of Creation, of all that is (aided by the natural setting of the retreat center) as coming from God, from His NAME, His Word... His Blessed Silence. I could sense His Silence at the heart of all, from which all springs, and so could see all things so much more clearly as all became illumined by His Word. Praise God! (May this vision stay with me always.)

March 5 – Complacency

Yesterday's enlightenment was with me in the morning (and when taking a moment in prayer), but seemed to dissipate during the course of the day.... I've often noticed that when a blessing comes, when things go right spiritually, I find myself subject to temptations, becoming unchristian in my attitude, if not falling into sin. Of course, these are the times the devil attempts to break us down, and if we are not aware of his workings but become inflated or complacent, a fall becomes likely.

The understanding of the Divine NAME that came yesterday was most important and must not be forgotten. It has me more than ever considering giving talks, one of which would address the Divine NAME. I put this idea into the Lord's hands and pray He will make it so, and done according to His will, if He so desires it. (But keep me ever humble, Lord.)

March 6 – Seek Ye First...

Another financial blessing as I realize while putting my mom's affairs in order, and talking to my wife, that I can put one of her stocks in my (and my brother's) name and then sell the stock... and it would be taxable income for me, something I need each year to be eligible for the ACA but which I expect to lack this year because of the likelihood of not teaching up north.

It has been truly, and repeatedly, remarkable how the Lord has taken care of me (and us) over many years – seek ye first the Kingdom of God....

March 7 – Children of God

Priest this morning spoke of how Christians are chosen as the Israelites were chosen, with a special blessing, and so are God's children. It seems in a sense an obvious thing, a teaching not unknown or uncommon, but the priest's explanation I found particularly enlightening for its simple honesty and truth. He did not shy away from separating Christians out, as Jesus did not shy away when He called members of other nations "dogs." There was nothing confrontational in the priest's words; as I say, just simple truth. For the central focus of his homily was our call to be as God, shining His love on the evil and the good, loving our enemies and calling them to become, with us, children of God, blessed as Christ. It is repentance that leads us all to the Lord and His blessing; and when we come there, we must be as He is.

March 8 – Transfiguration Sunday

That light I seemed to touch the other day in finding substantiation for belief in YHWH being the heart of the Bible and the heart of Creation – living in that light seemed within reach. The glory of God was upon me.

But, again, the distractions, even if not sinful, seem to keep me from that vision. What am I to do? What in my life belongs, is in the will of God, and what do I take up that may not be so blessed, that might be of my own will? All I can do is pray, is place the question before the Lord and honestly and openly seek His will, wherever it may lead. I pray it leads to transfigured glory, and most of all that I will find that glory, whatever cross may come.

HOME

March 9 – The Poorest

This is the feast day of St. Frances of Rome, whose service to the poor was unparalleled. Reading about her in the Office (and hearing the priest repeat the same reading during his homily), I remembered that it was repeated several times during our pro-life training a couple of days ago that we are Jesus' "hands and feet" in our service of the unborn and their mothers (and fathers). It seemed to confirm what I had wondered about a couple of weeks ago regarding how to serve the poor – it is true that these babies in danger of abortion are among the poorest of the poor.

March 10 – Infractions

The virus from China is obsessing the world, though it appears no worse, perhaps weaker, than others doing more damage. Masses are being cancelled, all Italy is shut down... and though cases have not been numerous here in the States, the media has people panicking. (Good for ratings.)

In this diocese we have the recommendation not to receive on the tongue, though it is not a requirement. I opened my mouth to receive on the tongue this morning, and at first the priest didn't give me Communion. I thought he just didn't realize I had my mouth open, and said "tongue"; he then relented, grudgingly.

He came to speak to me after Mass, suggesting I was being proud. But it was just out of habit I sought to receive on the tongue, and having been told hands are dirtier than mouths. But that seems not to be the case as I research the question. So I will likely begin receiving Communion in the hand until order is restored. But I find it ironic that a priest would question Communion for an infraction that at most put physical health at risk, but when it comes to spiritual health and proper reception by souls in a state of grace... there is seemingly no concern

How the media controls the population. It is a kind of slavery. Sad it also affects the Church. (The devil must be happy.)

March 11 – Watching Over

Sylvia's first day alone as sacristan, on the anniversary of her father's death. I find myself watching over her from a distance, much as perhaps her father is as well.

March 12 – China Virus

Today the seriousness of at least the reaction to the virus from China, which appears to be spreading worldwide, becomes clear. Already Italy had been shut down with no Masses even in Vatican City, and this morning I hear of a diocese in the US suspending all Masses. Then came news of two professional sports leagues suspending their seasons, colleges going remote throughout Florida, all Knights of Columbus events being suspended nationally, no nursing home visitations.... As I say, the reaction has become noticeably extreme and it seems it can only get worse. I pray Masses will not be suspended here, but some say it is only a matter of time.

Perhaps this scourge has come because of the state of a world enmeshed in a culture of death and promoting transgenderism even to children. Maybe the Lord has no other way but to send such a chastisement.

March 13 – Fortuitous Mistake

More peace, acceptant of whatever will be, whatever is...

Secretary set up a table for me in the church foyer, not realizing I wasn't scheduled to sell my books for a couple of weeks; but I found this to be a fortuitous error and realized it would be better to offer the books now, especially with all the church closings going on.

March 14 - Creative Silence

At church 4½ hours to set up and cover two Masses, selling books. Felt like less than two hours, which is about how much time I was able to spend in the chapel. And in a magazine I read of our union with God, which He so much desires and which we approach in prayer. (He is always waiting.)

And tonight catching part of a (romantic) drama I've seen before, in a scene with the man and woman dancing, her head on his chest, the camera circling slowly... there is a profound silence, a silence from which creation springs, new life. Here, too, in the embrace of husband and wife, the silence is spoken, the NAME of God is known. In such was man created, and woman from him, from the mud of the earth... and in such silence new life is conceived, in the union of man and woman, who image God, the Creator.

March 15 - The Depths

At church another five or six hours. Masses sparsely attended, even though it wasn't announced till this weekend the bishop has given dispensation from the Sunday obligation. (But pleased with number of books gotten into others' hands.)

"The cistern is deep." Line from the gospel of the Samaritan woman at the well, the utter outcast whom the Lord draws into Himself and who then evangelizes her whole town. And Jesus spent two days teaching these foreigners, these enemies of Israel, convicting them of the truth of His divinity.

Only Jesus can read the depths of our soul and tell us all we've done... and so set us free, free to receive the Holy Spirit.

It is He who speaks to you. Listen to Him in the depths of your heart.

March 16 – Reality

Impatient again with reactions and excessive precautions regarding the virus and its constant coverage... spurred by talk of losing Mass, but also the way hearsay gets around so fast.

Funny. Just recalled that is what the priest spoke about in what I thought was a rather mundane homily. People have expectations that don't match reality or the ultimate reality, which is God.

May He not find it necessary to take Himself (in the Sacrament) from us. This one thing let us keep, even if we fail to appreciate it fully; for where would we be without it? (Sometimes what seems mundane is the most necessary.)

March 17 – Work Is Food

Three and a half hours at Planned Parenthood despite not sleeping well and feeling very weak upon waking. Manage to make it out the door for early Mass, though remained tired throughout the morning – at Mass, adoration, and PP... till things became active there and potential saves arose. I then forgot all about lacking sleep and being weak, and ended up staying later than usual. Didn't realize the energy I'd found from such work till I arrived home.

We have food, Jesus tells us, and that food is to do the will of the Father, and that food nourishes us better than any bread; for man does not live by bread alone but by every word that comes forth from the mouth of God. May the Lord speak through us, always.

March 18 – No Trust

Masses suspended after tomorrow. Terrible news which I have difficulty understanding and accepting. It is like those who refuse the cup because of germs; there seems no trust, no faith. Judgments are made not by faith but by science, which again holds the trump card in this age.

HOME

Christ would not allow evil to come from the good of the sacraments.

March 19 – St. Joseph, Pray for Us

A day of genuine sorrow and just anger as the bishop not only suspends all Masses but closes all churches, going along with other bishops in the country. A truly sad state of affairs, a giving in to fear rather than a standing in faith, and a failure to realize the seriousness of the consequences as we put down the very spiritual weapons we should be zealously taking up at this time, closing up shop when we should be doing all we can within reason to stay open, and open all the time. Instead, reason escapes us, even as faith is set aside, and there is no sense of discovering creative solutions to supposed, if not imaginary, problems.

I'm afraid this scenario reveals all too clearly the worldly focus of most bishops in this country and the world. We need to pray more for our Church than for the virus.

St. Joseph, please pray for the Church of which you are Patron, that she will trust in her own resources. We consecrate ourselves to you this day.

(Woke last night unable to fall back to sleep, realizing this would be the last Mass for perhaps quite a while. Prayed Office of Readings in the night for the first time in a long while. Afterward reclined in a chair and felt peaceful as I tried to sleep. I thought of saints like Faustina whom the Lord had blessed with special graces... and as I lay there resting, it felt like the baby Jesus was in my arms.)

March 20 – Miracle Mass

Drove two hours to Orlando for Mass at a Maronite church. Also blessed with an hour of prayer before Mass and time to pray a Rosary after. It seemed a crazy thing to do, and upset my wife, but I found out about the Mass this morning and had time to make it,

March 2020

and since Mass has long been my #1 daily priority, I took off. And the ride really was not difficult.

How my heart rose as I took the exit and approached the church. The doors were locked but someone answered at the office and let me in, saying there would be one final Mass today because the pastor didn't have time to let people know otherwise. I was so grateful.

And so the seemingly impossible word I put faith in during prayer yesterday – that today I would somehow receive the Lord again – came to pass by the grace of God. And the banishment as of Romeo I felt yesterday, at least for one day is resolved, and I could meet my lover.

March 21 – Face to Window

After an early visit to a nearby Coptic Orthodox church, where Divine Liturgy was scheduled but (though one Egyptian member showed up for it) did not take place, I went over to our parish church for outdoor Stations, drive-through Confession... and a Rosary by a side door.

Through a window I could see the tabernacle (candle lit), as one door to the chapel was left open. I knelt there and prayed, moving closer and closer to the window till near the end of my Rosary my nose was pressed upon the glass. The closer I got, the clearer I could see the tabernacle and the closer I felt to Jesus inside. And the spiritual communion I sought was so real, I didn't mourn so badly about missing reception of the Sacrament for the first time in decades.

Later at Planned Parenthood was blessed in prayer to St. Joseph with instruction not to let my mouth flap so much but to be silent – O let it be so! – and realize the Lord's presence within me... and to remember the sky we look upon and the earth beneath our feet is the same sky Jesus looked upon and the same earth that was beneath His feet.

HOME

March 22 – Laetare Sunday

By a very special grace my wife and I were able to receive the Sacrament today and even spend a short time in a church praying the Rosary before the tabernacle. This is Laetare Sunday and we had good cause for rejoicing. But I fear a lack of gratefulness and appreciation for such a great gift. Nor do I carry through well with the cross such grace brings. Instead, I tend to wonder what tomorrow will bring.

O Lord, come back to us all!

March 23 – Outside

Sat outside in the driveway with my mom and wife after dinner. My mom has been especially cooped up. She doesn't go out much anyway, but hadn't stepped outside at all for over a week, not even as far as we did today, and has been listening too much to the media reports. I pray it helped relieve any tension and is something we can make a habit.

March 24 – Persistence

Persisted with witness at Planned Parenthood; still had a number of counselors come out, with a measure of success in our work.

As long as they stay open, despite the virus and the orders for elective procedures to cease, so long will we be out there. There is greater sense of dedication and sacrifice under the current circumstances. Pleased to see so many stand strong.

March 25 – Word from Our Lady

Back in prayer before the window looking in toward the chapel. Today I was there during (live-streamed) Mass and for adoration following. I could see but could not hear anything, so it was a bit like being deaf. Could follow other parts of the Mass, but was a little lost during the homily. Our Lady seemed to tell me then that the virus is not especially dangerous, that the risk was indeed being exaggerated, but that I should not speak out against others' fears but understand them and accept them. I realized this is what our Lord does with us in His patience regarding our sins. He forgives and even excuses us as He bears with our weaknesses. We must do the same.

March 26 – Stiff Neck

Today we had two hours of Eucharistic adoration at a church in a neighboring diocese that is keeping its doors open. A great blessing. We may go back on a regular basis if I can take the drive. Also had a blessed experience of the Mass (Communion following) with a beautiful homily by a priest friend featuring a call to repentance very much needed. I realized it is not just "others" who need to hear this blessed call more often from the pulpit: I do as well. We all do. More and more.

May the Lord forgive my stiff neck.

March 27 – Urbi et Orbi

Blessed to have made it back to the church with Eucharistic adoration, and to have a young man (with several children) play the Pope's Urbi et Orbi message and prayers in the church during our last hour. So, while the Pope was in adoration at St. Peter's, we were in adoration, too; and listening in we were able to receive the special plenary indulgence by praying for an end to the virus.

March 28 – Communion

A break, an opening in the local Church. The bishop has permitted parishes to give Communion (though no Mass and churches still closed). A few are doing so tomorrow, Sunday. My own pastor has spoken favorably of giving me (and my wife) Communion. And today he did so after the (live-streamed) Mass.

HOME

I can't thank the Lord enough for this grace, this great blessing, and the hope it brings. (I was inside the chapel itself for a few minutes, and it was like being home.)

March 29 – Sister's Mass

Got to stay in the foyer for Mass with my wife. Had time for Rosary before the Mass, and as I started praying a second Rosary afterward, the priests started a second Mass. I realized the intention would be for my sister, and so we stayed. It was a great blessing to be in attendance. When they read Lynn's name, Sylvia looked over at me and smiled. Then when I got home, the Knights were about to pray the Rosary together online. I just happened to tune in as they were beginning.

Very blessed opportunities for prayer.

March 30 – Video Help

Sylvia and I went up to the St. Petersburg church again for adoration. Didn't think I'd make it since I threw my back out yesterday and didn't sleep well. But woke feeling fine with back much better and got out on the road early as planned.

The priest arrived at the church the same time we did and asked if we had a cell phone to film him doing first day of consecration to St. Joseph (to finish May 1). I managed to do so and eventually to get him the video.

Heard a call from the Lord the other day to help this church; not sure if this was one way, or if this might lead to doing other videos, something a friend I'd contacted for help with transferring the video suggested and which I had wondered about myself.

Looks like it will be another month of closed churches, so will likely be visiting St. Pete rather frequently. We'll see where it leads.

March 31 – Gift

The pastor has been remarkably kind in allowing us to receive. I don't understand why no one else seems to ask him for the Sacrament. And so I wonder if I am being presumptuous. But my love of the Lord wins out over these fears (and I still pray outside the chapel door). My only real fear is lack of gratitude for such a great gift and a failure to join myself well to the Lord's sacrifice.

April 1 – Broad Brush

I woke sensing an end to this virus situation, but today the governor announced a stay-at-home order throughout Florida, even though the virus is bad only in one area of the state. Though regional plans had been suggested, still painting with a broad brush. Patience.

We also heard of the first person we know getting the virus, though it was not someone here but a nurse who works in NYC and takes the subway.

April 2 – All the Time

During two-hour adoration, while prostrate before the Lord, I was thinking, praying that someday I will be able to *live* with Jesus in the church, all the time, not having to drive forty minutes or ten minutes or even walk across the street to spend an hour or two (or even three) but live where he is near, accessible, with me, *always*. This is the dream. I think as I write this that it may have to wait till Heaven, but it is something possible in this world, where we have the tabernacle with us, where Jesus remains.

April 3 – Douay-Rheims

Took up rereading the Douay-Rheims version of the Bible a few weeks ago, just a few chapters a day during adoration time. Began Exodus today.

HOME

What a relief and what a pleasure it is to be able just to read the Bible, without having to deal with faithless commentary as I have had to do for years, if not decades. Not only is the language blessed with poetic reverence and clarity, but the commentary is actually faithful to the Church, faithful to the Word... and reasonable. What a grace!

Thank you, Lord.

April 4 – Passion

In the night there is darkness (and tears), but with the dawn comes rejoicing; and so it is with me today. After a fast yesterday and some difficulty sleeping, somehow I woke in joy, in light.

And after Confession, as I kneel and pray before the window that looks into the chapel and the tabernacle, I cannot see Our Lady in the corner (where I ordinarily kneel on Saturday after my Confession and pray a Rosary), but my longing is answered by a sense of kneeling not at the foot of a statue, but before Our Lady herself in Heaven. What blessings the Lord gives me!

And this evening Holy Week begins with the Passion of our Lord. I pray He continues to bless us with His presence, for if truly nothing matters but receiving Him, what should we not be ready to give for such grace – what should we not sacrifice?

April 5 – Sunday

Went to a nearby church (where we sometimes go for daily Mass) since they are the only one giving out Communion, though the bishop said parishes could. It seemed rather orderly: cars lined up, waited at a distance, then went forward near priest when the time came. People got out of their cars and walked over to the priest (behind an altar and with protective gear), then went back and drove away. The church is in a wooded area so there was enough space, though the line was out near the road when we left. Arrived a little early and pulled to the side to finish a Rosary with my wife before receiving, a peaceful moment of preparation.

Later went to parish church to pray a couple of Rosaries with my face pressed against the window looking on the tabernacle. Also, been trying to keep my mom occupied, so we played a game and sat outside a while. Tomorrow we'll be back to adoration in neighboring diocese.

April 6 – Memento Mori

Read an article encouraging *memento mori*, remembering our death, and indeed I woke in a bit of fear this morning, with some trepidation about setting out in the dark for our forty-minute highway drive to adoration. But this remembrance helped heal me of my rushing in the car, as I resolved to remain within five miles of the speed limit (instead of ten) and avoid the fast lane. One of my biggest struggles is driving with patience; in fact, the last ride to this church my wife complained several times about my speeding. I pray this is a breakthrough.

And the remembrance of death was accentuated by the gospel today as we find Lazarus seated at table with Jesus a week before our Lord's own death. But it must be said this passage emphasizes, too, the life that comes after death, for Lazarus has been raised... and our Lord shall be resurrected. We know that though all must pass through this portal, in Christ no one really dies but is brought to life. And this I remember as I look upon the clouds as we cross the Skyway Bridge on our way home.

April 7 – Witness

There was much trepidation approaching our weekly (abortion day) vigil at Planned Parenthood. Abortions go on despite government limitations to essential (medical) services, and so we find ourselves compelled to continue our witness as babies continue to die.

I received a letter from a pro-bono lawyer outlining our legal right to do our outreach despite the stay-at-home orders from the governor. But we had heard of those in like situations being

HOME

arrested in other states, so I suggested perhaps we should have a more limited witness.

A few stayed home, but our numbers were virtually the same – still very strong. And we were able to pray and hold signs and counsel without disturbance from the police... and at least one baby was saved.

There seems no stopping the abortion machine, whose business booms as most others suffer gravely. But by God's grace and Our Lady's intercession we still have a voice.

April 8 – Desert Time

Managed a pretty balanced bread fast on this last Wednesday of Lent. The Triduum is on the horizon. It will be a modified experience of these holiest days, but the Lord is looking out for us and I pray it will be a blessed time even though the Body of Christ cannot gather in large numbers.

I pray this desert time will convert many souls, and my own, to the Lord and His way. We all need to draw closer to Christ, but for the society as a whole great repentance is needed, and this is an opportunity, an act of God, that could help overturn the culture of death that so pervades the world. Those who continue to harden their hearts like Pharaoh in the face of the plagues (about which I read today) will have little hope of salvation.

O Lord, let your mercy pour forth,
and may souls be open to such grace.

April 9 – Spiritual Communion

For the first time I had a genuine sense of spiritual communion this evening during Holy Thursday Mass. After the priest gave repeated exhortation and encouragement of it in his homily, I did feel in union, in communion with the Lord. I had been downplaying its importance throughout this time of suspended Masses, and still would not want now to downplay the importance of actual Communion (for which there is distinct necessity, at least as long as we are human beings on this earth), for we must be really, physically united with our God, who became incarnate for our sakes... but I admit there is something essential to discover in spiritual communion. For if our Communion with our Lord is *only* physical, it becomes as transient, as passing, as the Jews' blood relation to the Christ. Our heart and soul, too, must be united with Him or our Communion is in vain.

April 10 – Good Friday

Fasted well on this day so made for fasting. Became conscious that I am a sinner, that, truly, all are sinners in the eyes of God but that He indeed has mercy on the soul that recognizes its sin (like the thief on the cross). And I seek in prayer to make my faith concrete, to realize the presence of the saints, and of course our Lord. At one point in my prayers I realize Peter truly existed and exists still, and I seek to speak with him.

Jesus walked the earth, was flesh and blood in our midst, and so were all those who followed Him. We must seek the *reality* of the Faith, and this starts with recognition of the sins of man and our own sins. For all His disciples abandoned Him.

April 11 – Jesus' Face

Yesterday during the Passion (and before in my reading), the Servant passage from Isaiah resonated in its speaking of Jesus having no stately bearing, nothing that would attract us to Him; and this morning in prayer (kneeling outside chapel window), I seemed to see the face of Jesus – not 'pretty', as it is often depicted, but simple, and strong. I thought of the Shroud of Turin and the Veil of Manoppello. And I came across two programs on the Shroud today, though I hadn't turned on the TV myself either time. And as I sat to write this I looked up, and on the kneeler in front of me was a small card with the face of Jesus from the Shroud and the Veil.

HOME

This sense of the Lord's face has served to make Him more real to me, humble and true, and strong.

The Lord is risen, Alleluia!

April 12 – "You Are Here"

A blessed Easter Day with both Communion and a fine meal.... And this morning I went over to the church to kneel and pray a Rosary at my 'perch' looking upon the tabernacle inside. No one around. (We have been experiencing a kind of extended Sabbath, giving rest to the land.) And on this Easter Sunday I find tears upon my face from the realization that Jesus is here alone; and I was filled again with an intense longing to be with Him, to stay with Him, always. It was a longing like that of Mary Magdalene led to the tomb, like the deer that thirsts for running streams.

As I stood up I said to Him, "You are here." But as I began to back away I heard Him tell me He is 'here,' within me. Still, as I drove home I prayed for both the opportunity to present itself wherein I could be with Him always (as a priest would be able to, or a monastic... or a Hermit of Bethlehem), and the courage to take that opportunity, to truly desire it. There is nowhere I'd rather be.

April 13 – Easter Monday

Out early to neighboring diocese for adoration again...

There is a certain Easter joy and peace upon me, and I find myself better disposed to avoid sin, especially that of impatience and unkindness. It is ironic that when we are in the midst of sin, we are hardly aware of it, or at least manage to ignore it. But when we come out of it, when we see ourselves acting as we should, with love toward others, in peace and patience... then we realize how far afield we have been. May the Lord continue to bless me with His peace, for it is by grace alone we overcome sin.

April 14 - Dark Day

This morning was so dark, so oppressively hot and humid and overcast. It was appropriately ominous for another day at the gates of hell. One could hardly breathe. And as we arrive at Planned Parenthood we hear terrible news of the return of a couple who had left so joyfully from the pregnancy clinic just two weeks ago.

Two communal Divine Mercy Chaplets today, one at PP and the other in a church, both in prayer for the terrible tragedy occurring still in abortion clinics. "Have mercy on us and on the whole world." How this prayer rings out at the gates of PP (indeed, as at the gates of hell), calling for mercy upon those entering there. May many be saved.

April 15 - He Hears

Since I always seem to forget (or doubt), it continually seems to surprise me when I find that the Lord answers prayers, though He always does. Yesterday I offered sincere prayers in conversation with the Lord regarding some health problems - stiff neck, sore shoulders... and by the end of the day, and noticeable especially today, I find relief (and jump for joy like the lame man healed in our first reading). I was able to sleep six or seven hours without waking, a considerable improvement on my waking every twenty minutes or hour the previous nights, and the longest I ever really sleep straight.

When we speak to Him, really talk to Him knowing He is listening, He hears all and is quick to respond. If only we had faith.

April 16 - Every Day

Today was one cold day amongst many particularly hot and humid ones, and so windows and doors were opened. But what came in this morning was not fresh air but the terrible stench of a dead animal, which I had to dispose of. It was not a pretty sight. (Left

HOME

me unable to eat for hours.) It marked a day on which, because of laziness on my part, we did not make it to adoration.

Every day is a new day to be cherished and *lived* in the Lord. Every day. It does not matter where we live or what we do, we cannot take a day off from serving God and doing His will. Lest we die.

This very day your soul is required of you.

April 17 – Special Blessing

How surprised we were when upon entering the church in neighboring diocese early this morning for adoration, the priest waved us over toward the sanctuary, indicated for us to kneel at the side altar, and gave us Holy Communion! What a special blessing.

The Lord has taken care of us in remarkable ways, making Communion available to us despite the current situation. And though we feel a little circumspect about such privilege, our love of the Lord and desire for the Sacrament lead us to accept such graces. May we express the thanksgiving we should for these favors from the Lord.

April 18 – Joy of Communion

Travelled a significant distance with hopes, expectations, we would be able to stand in the vestibule of a chapel during Mass... but were frustrated by a locked door, and even blocked windows. Waited outside for the forty minutes of the Mass, occasionally able to hear something of the priest's voice when the traffic stilled, not especially recollected. But when the priest came outside to give us Communion – all frustration, all sense of complaint, fled as the joy of union with the Lord took over. There really is nothing more important in this world.

April 19 – Divine Mercy

The Easter Octave is completed in the Mercy of the Lord, a mercy without which we would ever remain incomplete, lost, ourselves.

Since we brought our first-class relic of St. Faustina for the altar, we were blessed to attend a Divine Mercy Holy Hour wherein one of Vinny Flynn's daughters sang the chaplet. (The Lord also blessed us with Mass attendance at a distance.)

I am completing rereading of St. Faustina's *Diary* – about a page a day, so it has been with me a couple of years. She is now a few months from death, and the end of her suffering, and as she continually trusts in the Lord, she reaches new levels of union with Him.

But I can hardly trust that I will make my next appointment (though inevitably I end up with time to spare). How I yet need to open myself to the Lord's Mercy, as I seek to do today at the priest's exhortation.

April 20 – The Spirit of John

Specially blessed again today as we arrive early at church in neighboring diocese, and are again called to Communion before exposition of the Sacrament. And what a blessing it was to go directly from receiving Jesus to turning and seeing Him there in the monstrance... and then being able to spend two hours with Him. It elevated the prayer that followed, especially reading the beginning of Revelation in the Office.

John's words became so real that when the Lord told Him to write down the visions he was receiving and those he would later receive... I thought I could write in the spirit of John, so much did I put myself in his place while reading his account.

O to be truly a disciple, a missionary disciple, of the Lord, ready to give all over to Him, as I seek to do each morning in my waking prayer.

April 21 - His Miraculous Presence

Another blessed day. For the first time we are invited into a church proper for at least part of a Mass, most notably the consecration. It brought tears to my eyes. It also brought intense intercession for a save at Planned Parenthood, from whence we had come; and when we returned we found there had indeed been a turnaround!

We do not deserve the blessings the Lord showers upon us (as my wife says), but each day, at least of late, I seek to live in His miraculous presence and do His will. May this resolve continue to the end of my days. (It feels so much like Easter this year.)

April 22 - Virtual Mass in Church

The poignant moment of today came in an unexpected way. During our adoration time I went to the back of the church to watch the live-streamed Mass of our parish. Questioned somewhat whether it would take away from adoration and so if I should wait till later for virtual Mass.... But it turned out to be a moving experience. There was nothing special about the Mass itself, but viewing it in a church with Jesus exposed on the altar elevated everything and brought it closest to being an actual Mass. As I say, it was very unexpected, but undeniable in the effect it had on me. A holy moment.

April 23 - White Car

Switched black (long-term rental) car for white one of the same make and model. Seemed wise, especially since summer weather is upon us here in Florida; and appropriate also now that we have entered Easter Season and the virus hysteria seems to be abating, with talk of things opening up.

I had met an Enterprise employee in the parking lot of our church a few weeks ago; he was looking for our pastor, to whom I introduced him, in order to get permission to use the church lot for their overflow cars. A few days ago my wife and I noticed the car (color) we'd wanted in the lot, and so arranged the change. (The same employee helped us today. His name is Emmanuel and he was born on Christmas Day.)

And in my exercise to regain health, felt strong for the first time in a while running on the elliptical machine. Perhaps a new day is dawning.

April 24 – Stations in the Rain

Stormy weather dissuaded me from travelling to St. Pete for adoration this morning, but I suppose if I had found the faith and courage to go I would have missed praying my Stations in the rain at our parish church.

The rain had considerably slowed when my wife and I headed over to the window to pray an hour near the tabernacle. I could have done my Stations then (dry) but forgot until we had already started a Rosary. Prayed another Rosary, but it was still coming down hard, so I set out in the pouring rain to walk the outdoor Stations. I had an umbrella, and it slowed to a steady rain about halfway through, but it was still a special blessing, one which I prayed would serve to cleanse me of my sins, and temporal punishment for them.

April 25 – Trembling for Sinners

Back at my window again praying alone after Confession, I do my best to open myself to the Lord and His Word. And as I begin to think of those sinners who move my heart toward anger and remember that I must love my enemies... I seek to do so. At first I prayed for those truly suffering from the current virus and to take their pain upon myself. It was difficult. But then I turned my heart to those terribly immersed in the culture of death, and taking their pain was overwhelming, causing me to tremble to my bowels and moan for the help of Mama Mary. So much darker is sin than disease. But we must be as Jesus and take all on ourselves if we are to be Christians.

April 26 – Online Rosary

Prayed the Rosary with fellow Knights of Columbus and their families through an online program. Have done so the past few Sunday mornings (after online Mass and Communion at a nearby church). I suppose it serves as a prayer group through which one could gain a plenary indulgence (for praying Rosary together). Would have found such an idea suspect, but it has been a blessing, a time of peaceful prayer, and another sign of the Lord's presence with us in ways we might not have thought.

April 27 – Encouragement

Gave a couple of my books to pastor of the church in St. Petersburg. He spoke well of them and said he would use prayers from one in weekly bulletin. It was a blessing to have such encouragement, but the most encouraging thing is the availability of adoration and Communion. How does one thank someone for that gift?

April 28 – Red Day

The feast of St. Louis de Montfort, yes, but also of St. Peter Chanel, a remarkable martyr who brought the faith to those who had never heard of the Lord. And in the readings we hear of St. Stephen, the first martyr of the Church, who died so much like Christ.

I look at my red rosary beads today and think about the four colors of the Church and how the other three (green, white, and violet) have seasons of their own but red has no season but except the blood of the martyrs, their feast days. And I realize this is as the eternal season coursing through all seasons, through all the Church, as blood itself, giving life to the Body.

And I recall now that it was on the feast of St. Stephen some fifteen years ago I first took to wearing a shirt the color of the day.

April 29 – Churches Opening

We hear today of our bishop allowing the opening of churches for prayer, which is very good news; unfortunately he has apparently prohibited adoration. So the question will be whether or not to continue traveling to St. Pete for adoration (as we do today and plan on doing at least the next couple of days) or settle for time before the tabernacle. Hopefully things will open more so soon... but at least there is another crack in the wall.

St. Catherine, pray for us.

April 30 – Monasteries

I recall thinking a while back that the U.S. could be a place made for monasteries, if not hermitages, because of its characteristic independence, and I wondered what American monastery life might look like. I still wonder, but it seems we have had a chance to experience it in these weeks dominated by the virus and people having to stay at home, many alone. Perhaps something will grow out of it. I pray more souls will at least turn to God and find His Silence speaking in their hearts.

May 1 – St. Joseph

On this feast of St. Joseph the Worker we drive to a parish of his namesake for our two hours of adoration. This parish has become our home away from home, and the pastor has been very kind. Had thought this might be our last ride to St. Petersburg, since churches open in our own diocese next week (and since today we had to give up our rental car and so drive again our ordinary vehicle, which has now received its recall repairs), but the pastor mentioned to us that Mass will return there shortly! So now we still have reason to take the ride up, even as traffic increases.

St. Joseph, pray for us; watch over and guide us.
Bless the Church of which you are Patron,
and which is reconsecrated to Mary today.

HOME

Thank you for all the graces that come through you.

May 2 – The Threshold

A psalm verse that has been on my mind throughout the current situation is the one that says, "I would rather stand at the threshold of the house of my God than dwell in the tents of the wicked" (84:10), for I have been continually on the threshold of the Lord's house. It seems that will soon change, but as it is, today I kneel again at the window looking into the chapel to do my Holy Hour, to pray a couple of Rosaries. And when I have been able to enter the house, it is in the vestibule I have found my place.

But I would rather kneel at this threshold than be in any other place on earth.

May 3 – Grace

A Sunday and so feast of Sts. Philip and James not celebrated. But a thorough Sunday: prayer, virtual Mass, Communion, Rosary with Brothers online, two Rosaries at my window outside the chapel, games with mom and wife, posting podcasts, more prayer, exercise... Let us move with the Spirit of God in all things.

I miss daily Mass terribly, but I do not think there is anyone more blessed than we have been to receive Communion every day since the end of the first week of this lockdown. It is impossible to express the grace it has been, and I do a poor job of thanksgiving.

May 4 – No Window

The churches opened today in our diocese and we went to two of them: a nearby one where we are blessed to be able to adore the Lord (and so didn't need to travel to St. Pete); and our parish chapel, where we later prayed a Rosary. To be inside looking at the tabernacle close up with no window between was blessed, but it was kneeling at the foot of the statue of Mary where I shed tears.

May 2020

And the Lord's face came to me this morning, beginning when I felt a sense of the betrayal of Judas and realized Jesus was not disturbed when He told His traitorous apostle to do what he was going to do quickly, but still possessed only love. (He lays down His life freely, and He takes it up again.) Seeing and knowing and remembering the face of Christ is key to knowing the Lord Himself. And it helped me know myself better, in its light.

May 5 – Ear to the Door

Mom's birthday. Another two saves at PP. Holy Hour... Thoughts/prayers regarding the importance, the blessing that is purity.

But perhaps the highlight of the day was experiencing Mass at a threshold again, just outside the glass doors of a shore church. When I placed my ear directly on the crack between the doors, I could hear the Mass. And I could also see inside if I shielded the sun with my hand. My wife could not hear but knew where we were by my responses, and so was able to respond as well. And we again receive Communion, which lights up our faces despite the circumstances.

One thing I've realized is that home is where Jesus most is. He is most with us in the Sacrament, and we are most blessed by the Sacrament when we receive it. We are also very blessed simply to be in His presence; and seeing Him exposed on the altar we are closer to Him than when He remains in the tabernacle. Thus, though our own parish chapel is our special home, we go to the nearby church for Holy Hour because it has adoration.

May 6 – Masks

I have managed to avoid wearing a mask throughout this situation, but to enter any of the now-open churches it is required, so I have to comply. I don't like to do so because it seems to exacerbate the problem, making people more fearful and showing a lack of trust in God. Also, in church it seems particularly inappropriate. I think of the Lord's proscription against men wearing hats in His

HOME

presence, and a mask seems likewise to hide the glory of God, indeed masking our faces before the Lord. We should be face to face in prayer. (But I suppose at least others can't see my dumb expression.)

There are so many masks we need to remove. I indeed pray today that the Lord make known the truth to me, that I might see any way in which I am lying to Him or to others, or myself. May He take away any blinders to such lies and bring me into His truth, whatever the cost, for this is most essential.

May 7 – "You Are My Tabernacle"

During a mundane time of waiting, the Lord touches my heart deeply.

My wife was late picking me up after my prayer, so I waited in the chapel for her. Actually, I went down the hall to the church, where I could better see the door. I realized at one point I was very unaware of Jesus' presence in the tabernacle, so I tried to focus my attention on Him, and uttered a little prayer to enter into the tabernacle to be with Him. This led to a sense that He was with me, present in me. First it was in my head He seemed to dwell; then later, waiting outside the door to the chapel (after having checked the parking lot for my wife), I felt Him dwelling in my whole body. I remembered the word He had given me some time ago: "You are my tabernacle," and I prayed very hard to be, and to remain, His tabernacle, carrying Him with me wherever I go. But how pure one must be to be so.

This comes to me on a day when my sins rise to my eyes and I realize how much I need to purify my perverse and polluted, proud heart and soul. O Lord, let it be so.

May 8 – Purity

In the first words I come upon today in my continuous reading of the Bible during adoration, the Lord exhorts us to be holy as He is holy. It is from Leviticus, which has challenged my soul of late with its strong precepts, particularly as regards purity. And just before writing this, in my continuous daily reading of St. Faustina's *Diary* I came upon a passage on the glory of virgins and their incomparable blessings in Heaven (of which John spoke in Revelation (in the Office) recently).

But I am not pure. I am certainly not a virgin. Though I may have tasted this gift at times in my spiritual journey, it is not mine to know – this song I shall not be blessed to sing. But what purity I can find, I beg the Lord to provide.

And today I confess at a different parish, where penitents are offered Communion immediately afterward. If I were to confess well and receive well, could there be any better means to purity, any better preparation for death?

May 9 – Body of Christ

No vocal prayer is permitted in this initial week of an open chapel, but no one else was present so my wife and I were able to crown Our Lady (with a crown my wife made) with some prayers, followed by a Rosary. Someone came in just as we finished the Rosary, so I went over to the church to pray my Stations, so as not to distract anyone. Thought I'd return to the chapel for my second Rosary, but stopped in front of the tabernacle in the church to pray, no one else around.

Always a blessing to have a church or chapel to oneself, and so it was today, both in the crowning prayers with my wife and the Rosary alone in church, during which time I again recalled the Lord's profound word: "You are my tabernacle." I could not believe it could be so, but the word had power since it was spoken over me by Jesus, effecting what it proclaimed.

And it led to a further thought, a further realization – that being a tabernacle is wonderful, but one could think of the tabernacle as just a container. Better to be what the tabernacle contains. Better to be the Body of Christ Himself! And this is what the gospel spoke of today, of our being one with Jesus as He is one with the Father, of our doing His work, or rather His doing that work through us. A marvelous thing I pray will be so with my life, especially my prayer.

May 10 – Mother's Day

It was a rather mundane but very blessed day. My mom in tears thanks us for such a beautiful day, though all we did was play a game with her, go for a walk and sit with her in the driveway... then picked up some food. (She also got brief visits from my sister-in-law and her daughter.) She said every day is like Mother's Day with us.

I realized soon after that it should be me that is in tears, thanking the Lord for another blessed day, for indeed every day I am blessed to be with Him. Today He provides a Mass through our window, drive-through Communion, and a Holy Hour back at the window... then a Rosary online with my Brothers this afternoon.

A blessed day. Every day, indeed, it is true. And I do cry.

May 11 – MASS!

First bona fide public Mass in a couple of months as we drive early this morning up to St. Petersburg, where daily Mass returned today. It was a blessing, certainly, but I can't wait for the bishop in our diocese to allow its return. I can't see driving up in our aging car every day, especially when possibilities for Communion and adoration exist close by.

May the Lord guide the bishops' discerning the return to Mass; may He give them the faith and true reason they need. And may He continue to guide us on our path to Him each day.

May 12 – The Long and Winding Road

Got word today that Mass will return to our own diocese next Monday (18th), including Sundays. Prayed so hard for our bishop's

May 2020

faith and courage, and such a blessing to have these prayers answered. Though there are blessings in struggle, very much looking forward not to have to determine travel plans day to day in prayer, not knowing if I discern correctly. A good exercise, I suppose, but one which has resulted in much driving, generally an occasion of sin for me.

Didn't drive to St. Pete today but spent even more time in the car, going from adoration in one church to Planned Parenthood to Mass outside a door in another church (forty minutes away) and back to PP... then home. Has been a long and winding road, one I pray leads to our home in Heaven.

Let us stir into flame God's precious gift of eternal life.

May 13 – Mom

Spent some time with my mom today, something I should be doing more of, and for which the current situation has provided opportunity but which I have not taken advantage of as I should.

She turned 92 last week and has been locked in the house almost all of the time, and so has been getting more anxious (watching the news doesn't help). Over the weekend her sister was in the hospital and my cousin told me it didn't look good. Hearing that her sister wasn't well caused her to ask her doctor for a rather strong anxiety medicine (something I didn't know she'd done till today). So even more so should I be spending time with her. And who knows how much more time we will have together. It should be a priority.

On this feast of Our Lady of Fatima, let me remember my mom.

May 14 – Yellow Roses

Took my wife to lunch in a nice restaurant; we were the only customers. Earlier rode to St. Pete for Mass and Holy Hour on this the feast of St. Matthias and our 15th anniversary. Later played games with my mom, an enjoyable time. Also walked with

HOME

mom, and watched a good film with my wife. For the limited circumstances under which we operate, it was a good day.

Gave my wife yellow roses, which opened up so wide, wider and bigger than any roses I have ever seen. We all remarked how wonderful they looked. (My mom said they didn't even look like roses.) I think it was a sign of my love for my wife. I hadn't bought flowers for her in years, though previously I had done so regularly. (She asked me not to anymore, and I complied.) But when I bought these flowers I just knew they were something special; I was drawn directly to them and picked them up immediately. (Yellow is the devotional color for the Blessed Mother in my wife's region of the Philippines.) In fact, a couple of people complimented them as I left the store. And they had a wonderful scent, something that has seemed lacking in flowers in recent years.

May the scent come into the nostrils of the Lord and Our Lady as a blessed offering of love.

May 15 – Answered Prayer

A simple (and maybe a little selfish) but sincere prayer is answered today. And I knew it would be. And I promised if it were, I wouldn't doubt the Lord's ability to answer (sincere) prayer anymore. He does answer prayer. Everyone, at least every believer, knows that. Maybe I am the only forgetful soul who keeps seeking confirmation of the obvious.

And we take my mom for Confession and Communion today, and spend a little time with her sitting by the water. She appreciated it, especially Confession and Communion. And so the Lord answers another prayer.

May 16 – What Doesn't Pass

The news is that my aunt is dying, my mom's last sibling. I cannot tell her. She feels so bad that she is the eldest and all her brothers and sisters have gone before her. I think my brother and I should be together to tell her when the time comes.

But it is another blessed day of prayer and receiving Communion (with mom again)... and this evening we watch a replay of the Lightning winning the Stanley Cup sixteen years ago in a Game 7. But all things are passing. None of these things that seem to matter will last. Not one stone will be left upon another. And will we still be blessed? I pray so. More blessed.

Sitting alone before the tabernacle, I feel the urge to write. Though I have a pen, there is nothing to write on since everything (books, bulletins, envelopes, etc.) has been removed from the church. I then find a call to write on my heart, with my flesh and blood... with my life instead of with words on paper, which indeed pass away. (As this shall.)

May 17 - Christ in Me

Woke this morning singing Paul's refrain: "No longer I but Christ who lives in me" (Gal.2:20), and in speaking my sins before the Lord, not lying, not saying I have no sin but confessing that I am perverse and polluted... the Lord seems to reach down to me and pick me up - and indeed I feel as though He lives in me, for I reject my sin and accept His grace and mercy.

The priest speaks of this sense in his homily, of how God is closest to us in our weakness; if we bow humbly under His mighty hand, He will raise us up.

And in my last time outside the window looking into the chapel, I pour sweat as I kneel and pray the Sorrowful Mysteries on this hot day, praying as if for the first time for the victims of the current virus, realizing that though it may be overblown, there are people truly suffering and dying, as always there are. How I have lacked compassion for their suffering! But the Lord blesses me with it today as I give myself to Him and to His sacrifice. May He indeed live in me.

May 18 – MASS RETURNS!

Mass returns to our diocese! Masks, distancing, 25% capacity... but still Mass. And Mass every day. No more ad hoc managing of schedule to at least be able to receive Communion and fulfill Holy Hour. Mass available every day. And adoration available, too, Monday to Friday, not yet at own parish but in nearby church. And I think things will quickly get back to normal, as that seems the way it is going. As all of a sudden, in a matter of days, everything was shut down, now things are returning to normal as fast. Praise God!

I believe it is fear that has been the principal problem, a fear that comes from not knowing God, who is love, and whose love casts out all fear, especially fear that is unwarranted.

May 19 – Still Greater Progress...

Praying and witnessing to the font of salvation at Planned Parenthood today, 3 1/2 hours in the sun and heat and humidity... But perhaps such a purgatory is necessary for my perverse and polluted soul.

I recall my sins this morning, my sins that led to my conversion, to my two years of tears considering especially the ways in which I failed my little sister. But I was ignorant, Lord, though now I am not. You have forgiven me my sins, but still my heart is not pure, still I need your chastisement – still I am a sinner. O let me not forget how far I have fallen, and how far I have yet to go to reach your glory, your presence in Heaven. Save me!

May 20 – Everyday Miracle

Sometimes the miracle is present just in an ordinary day.

Nothing really comes to mind as I consider the day, yet it was another blessed day, as is any day with Mass and adoration, prayer and work and rest with family. And perhaps this is the most significant lesson: that life itself, the seemingly mundane day-to-day activities (done with the Lord in mind), is a miracle. Life is a miracle for God is life, Life itself.

In Him we live and move and have our being. O that we could see this! (It would be a beatific vision, wherever we are.)

May 21 - Ascension Thursday

Should be Ascension Thursday, but not in this diocese. One of my least favorite changes in the Church - really seems it must be on Thursday, as the name commonly says, and as the nine days of prayer, the first novena, demands. (Always dreaded visiting Florida at this time; in NJ Thursday remains the day.}

Priest this morning thought we were celebrating Ascension today (retired priest who probably is usually back north by now). He spent some time searching for the gospel for the feast before someone told him... and he had prepared his homily for the feast, so went through with it anyway. Can't say I minded. How blessed it would be if the day were returned to its rightful place and we could celebrate it properly.

May 22 - A Peaceful Death

I realize today by practice how remembering the NAME of God (YHWH) can, and should, be done in all things, as it seems to solve a longstanding problem. It was a grace that I was placed into the LORD's Silence and so found clarity and blessing; and I pray I shall seek, and find, that grace more often... always... especially at the hour of death.

My aunt died today. I pray the peace of the LORD be upon her and she be carried in that peace to His arms. There is no more important moment to remember and be in the peace of Christ than at the hour of our death. If we are so, all will be well. (And my cousin tells me she indeed died peacefully.)

May 23 – Kneeling before Our Lady

After Confessions had ended I was left completely alone in the chapel for my Rosary kneeling before Our Lady and our Lord. This continues to be a most blessed time of prayer, of intimacy with Mary and Jesus in the tabernacle. I suppose it is mainly because I am coming from Confession and so possess a clean soul. But it is a devotion unmatched and very cherished. Thank you for such grace, O Lord.

May 24 – Blessings upon Bishops

Ascension celebrated today (Sunday).

Prayed before the tabernacle and the crucifix that any graces the Lord might give me be bestowed upon others, for so many graces, whether it be wisdom or anything else, I am afraid I waste.

O Lord, I pray especially the bishops be blessed, and I am sorry I have spent more time critiquing them than praying for them... as I do again today. Let the gifts of your Spirit pour upon all souls, especially those most influential.

May 25 – The Gifts of God

Thinking, praying again about the gifts the Lord pours upon me and how little used they are. Perhaps my prayer bears fruit for the Kingdom, but what of my knowledge, my wisdom and insight regarding Scripture and other spiritual matters? This mostly goes into books that nobody reads.

During this Pentecost Novena I continue to pray for the gifts of God to be poured upon those who can make use of them, that I be divested of them, that whatever I have be shared with others so they may bear fruit and not rot on the vine.

May 26 – Universal Holiness

After prayer, while holding a sign at Planned Parenthood, I enter into conversation with the Lord. He asks if what I am doing is useless. I admit that it isn't, and sense what He is trying to say. I explain that I wasn't referring (in the past two entries) to pro-life work, or prayer, or any other good work, just lack of employment of whatever wisdom and insight He might be giving me. While explaining, I realized that there are a lot of people who are gifted with spiritual knowledge today – I have conversations all the time with those well-versed in Scripture and the Faith – and that this is a sign of the Universal Call to Holiness coming to pass in our midst. And so, I am not alone – each has his own understanding to share, and it need not be on a large scale. (The large scale is made up of a multitude of small scales.) And so I apologize to the Lord for being overhasty in my words.

May 27 – Mom's Anxiety

My mom's been more anxious since her sister's death, so my wife and I have been trying to spend more time with her. Not always doing that as well as we could, though. (It hasn't helped that her TV has been going black for about a week.) Today was first time in close to a week I went for a short walk with her; but we have been playing board games with her almost every day. We have to take her out tomorrow, somewhere.

Still wondering about my own health – shortness of breath, pain in shoulders and arms, stomach problems... All seem to go together.

May 28 – Frustration

Finding it difficult to take care of my mother. I don't mind setting aside writing work and other things, but just don't know what to *do* or not – specifically, to take her to a restaurant or not, when, where... or outside somewhere in this terrible heat. I ended up slamming my fists on the desk in frustration, and things really aren't that bad yet. Very concerning. It turned out my wife just took her for a ride downtown, and that seemed to make her happy. I suppose the answer is simpler than I make it out to be. I seem to have no trust regarding these matters, in myself or in God (to whom I did pray for guidance).

May 29 – Waiting

Gradually getting back to normal. Mass returned to the church today at our parish (had been in the hall), and I lectored while Sylvia served as an extraordinary minister of Communion. Also, adoration returns to the parish in a few days... so bouncing over to nearby church won't be necessary. Can't wait till masks are not required any longer – I've already started taking mine off for periods of time during adoration, when far apart from others.

My mom is waiting for the clubhouse to open so she can play cards and bingo with her friends... but for now we continue to play games with her every day; and we walked this evening and sat out in the driveway for a good while.

May the Lord bless and guide the reopening of society and hasten the virus' demise.

May 30 – Move Closer

Specially blessed again in prayer before Our Lady after Confession: half a Rosary kneeling in front of her statue, other half a few feet over facing the tabernacle.

The intimacy here is always very intense, and it was so today. During fourth mystery (Transfiguration) I put my head to the ground, and I sensed how much I lack readiness to witness the Lord's transfiguration (or be transfigured myself). It then felt as if Our Lady, who was to my left (slightly behind), was praying over me.... I also sensed St. Joseph praying at my right, readying me for transfiguration.

As I began the last mystery (Institution of the Eucharist), I felt Mary encouraging me to move closer to the tabernacle. I was hesitant to step up (the one step, on my knees) into the sanctuary, but when I turned around a moment and saw that there was now no one else in the chapel, I did so. And as I prayed the mystery, I could not but mourn all the times I have received the Lord without appreciating the greatness of this gift, especially during the shutdown period. But again I was consoled by Our Lady (and our Lord), and my sorrow brought cleansing and health to my soul.

(Should note I find confirmation of the words I receive when I hear the devil's voice mock the messages.)

May 31 – Pentecost

Rather overwhelmed by the powerful, Spirit-filled readings today. The Spirit is so powerful that He joins peoples of all nations together as one to praise the glory of God; and in that praise all else falls away, nothing else matters but the Lord and His grace upon our souls. Alleluia!

What joy there is in the praise of God – how we then join with the angels and approach our Heavenly home with all the saints. We are freed from all our bonds and dwell in glory, all as one.

O Lord, fulfill what you began this day;
may the voices of your Church
all be raised in praise of your holy Name!

June 1 – Mary, Mother of the Church

A new and blessed feast celebrating the Church and our Mother on Monday after Pentecost... but unusual in that it is only a memorial yet obligatory – so no St. Justin today – and has its own readings.

But the readings are perfect: Mary amongst the apostles praying for the coming of the Spirit (and so the birth of the Church); and Jesus entrusting Mary to John, who stands for the Church as a whole. And water and blood flow from the pierced side of our Savior, symbolizing Baptism and Communion, the most essential sacraments of the Church.

HOME

O Mother, may the Church be blessed!

June 2 – Calvary

No saves at Planned Parenthood for a few weeks. One begins to blame oneself, for lack of prayer, lack of faith... failure to trust in the Lord, to put all in His hands.

This is such difficult work. We should be there as at a funeral; more so, as at Calvary witnessing the crucifixion of Christ. But who can be so conscious of the reality of what happens here each week?

Brought new crucifix (attached to a long 2 x 4) today, after I dropped, and thus smashed, the previous one a couple of weeks ago. Hopefully it helps remind us where we are.

June 3 – Martyrs' Joy

What do we say about suffering? Do we embrace it? Do we cherish it? I don't. But I should. It is what makes us Christians. What have we to offer if we have no suffering, no suffering in which we find a treasure?

In these first five days of June there are four martyrs' feasts. (The month ends similarly.) These souls knew the value of suffering and embraced it with joy, and so found the grace at its core.

But I fear every ache and pain and try to avoid every heartache. And I don't seem to get any better, even in small ways. I do nothing but complain. May the Lord save me, especially at the hour of death.

June 4 – Mercy for the Miserable

Finished St. Faustina's *Diary* today, after two years of reading a page or two a night. She ends speaking of the silence of God. But

June 2020

of course her main message is mercy, and that the most miserable sinners are those most embraced by our merciful Lord.

I cannot think of a more miserable sinner in this day than the police officer who killed a man lying on his belly, his hands cuffed behind his back, by kneeling on his neck for eight minutes as he pleaded for mercy; the last three minutes the man had become motionless. (It has been much in the news recently since there was clear video footage, and protests have followed.)

One's first reaction is condemnation – certainly of the act, but also of the perpetrator. But this is just the soul who needs God's mercy more than anyone. He is living in Hell and Satan has his heart. There is no greater misery than that.

Perhaps his sin is so deadly, perhaps his heart is so hardened, that prayers cannot help. But always we must hold out the hope Christ offers on the Cross: "Forgive them, Father, for they know not what they do." We hold this hope even for the architects of the culture of death. And so we pray: Lord, may all souls turn to you for mercy.

(Said, "God bless you, brother!" to a black man eating at the counter today as I left a restaurant with pizza in hand. He responded with thanks.)

June 5 – Rain

Another red (martyr's) day, and First Friday.

Blessed with a good fast and the grace to go from work to work, prayer to prayer, without becoming lazy. Also spent some good time with my mom, including a walk around the block between rainfalls. As we neared the end of our walk it began to rain, and we had no umbrella... but my mom made it home OK. She is still pretty strong.

It has been raining regularly for a few days. But the violence of the recent protests seems to be quelling. Into each of our lives rain must fall; as Paul tells Timothy today, a Christian will undergo persecution, but Jesus is there to save.

HOME

June 6 – Lasting Graces

Praying Joyful Mysteries in chapel after Confession, admitted to Our Lady that I couldn't be even a little bit like her... and this admission opened me up to sharing in the graces of each mystery, her consolation aiding the graces along. I was particularly concerned that whatever graces might come would quickly pass and so amount to nothing – again anxious about wasting blessings. I hope it is not so but that whatever dew of the Spirit was upon me in this intimate time of prayer has a lasting effect, even if I so soon become distracted.

(When I went out for the mail today an elderly couple married seventy-two years, who live down the street but have been staying in the house across from us while their place has been undergoing renovations after severe water damage, were getting into their car. I called to the man, asking if his house was almost ready, and he said they were on their way back there. I said, "Home, sweet home," and he responded, "There's no place like home!")

June 7 – Images

Watched a replay of the '69 Super Bowl between the Jets and the Colts, which I remember seeing when I was only eight. I was expecting the images to be ghostly, grainy, very unclear, but somehow, because it is film and not video I suppose, the picture seemed remarkably *real*. It was as if I could feel the mud and the grass; and the players looked like human beings. Something there is more real, more human, about film, something that is lost in our tremendously advanced digital imagery.

Yet there is something sort of frightening about the reality of it. What does it mean? What of these images that so dominate our culture? To what extent are they the idols of our age, the false gods? Certainly there is something that leans in this direction, a distinct temptation in the medium. What to make of it? A caveat, at least.

June 2020

June 8 – Reality and Humility

Had a kind of conversation with the Lord about images, film especially. Two problems were defined: first, it is essentially unreal. It gives the appearance of reality, but is not reality. Second, it engenders adulation. The images on the screen are easily made into "gods" to which people aspire. And so it certainly can be seen as the false idol of our age.

But is it inherently evil? Should it be abandoned, or can it be manipulated for good? The unreality will always be there, and the temptation to exalt it as well (and so avoiding it could be wise), but can these problems be overcome and utilized for holy ends?

We seem to know that it can, since we have all experienced the blessing of a good film (or work of art in another medium). Perhaps the unreality is overcome by pointing to a greater reality, a transcendent reality. And perhaps the pridefulness of it all can be conquered by a clear self-contempt. And so the film that points to God and is done in all humility may be a grace.

June 9 – Patience

Patience tested by those obsessed with the wearing of masks – a parishioner complains, a priest preaches from the pulpit... and meanwhile the WHO recants on its earlier proclamation that those without symptoms can spread the virus. And in the meantime, no one has symptoms, no one is sick, yet everyone must wear masks in church. It indeed continues that I know no one who has gotten sick here in Florida, but I know many who suffer the anxiety of isolation and fear.

I have tried to accommodate those who are fearful, and continue to do so; but one wonders where the line is drawn, and when faith and reason will kick in, at least in the Church.

Patience. Patience. For it, and love, I pray to Our Lady.

June 10 – Hands in Prayer

While in chapel praying before Mass (which is in the church), I began coughing. This morning I had gotten a small piece of overcooked (hard) pita bread stuck in my throat and couldn't seem to clear it. But it wasn't until church time I began coughing.

Was concerned not only for the few people in the chapel looking askance at me (coronavirus fears still abounding), but what I'd do if unable to get control before Mass. Our Lady called me up to her statue, and I stood there finishing my Rosary. I looked directly at her, and especially noticed her hands clasped in prayer. The control (and peace) I sought came almost immediately and remained with me through Mass (though I had to keep mostly silent).

Looking at Our Lady's hands in prayer reminded me of a time I prayed before a similar statue (the one on the cover of *Prayers to the Saints*). I was with my friend from The Gambia and just started crying uncontrollably as I felt the Blessed Mother speaking to me so intimately and so clearly, a deep, prophetic call upon my soul.

June 11 – Caregiving

Someone said the other day there is no greater work than caregiving; though it is something that should come naturally, it doesn't in this age. I didn't think of myself much when he mentioned it because my mom has been able to care for herself for the most part. But today I thought about it, and realized this is also a part of giving up my life to do the Lord's work. Had considered my writing and pro-life work and prayers in this way, but not so much caring for my mom... perhaps because we have also benefitted from being here (enabling us to do the other things).

But today I had to deal with my mom not feeling well (showing anxiety), setting up a new TV for her, and taking her to the ear specialist (who said one hearing aid does not work – the other she recently lost)... and it became a bit overwhelming.

More and more, it seems, caregiving will be a big part of our lives. I pray I put it in the Lord's hands.

June 12 – Light All Around

Ordered affordable hearing aids for my mom – hope the choice will be blessed.

Light is all around. It reflects the glory of God, His presence. If we have eyes to see.

I pray each day as I finish my face time, as I rise from my knees and stand before the Lord, that somehow as I leave I will still be with Him, that He will still be with me, throughout my day. How this can be I do not know, except by faith. And except by the light that is all around us always (as it is on this page now).

June 13 – St. Anthony

I seem to have more affinity with St. Anthony than I realized. Always appreciated his gentleness and innocence – for which I prayed before his statue every day in a former parish that bears his name (where the statue of Our Lady referred to above stands) – but was not as aware of his preaching ability and especially his sermons. I read that he compiled a book of homilies not unlike my own, St. Anthony's Bread, if you will. And so I will more so seek his blessed intercession. (Should also mention I go to his statue in our current parish each day before beginning Stations.)

June 14 – Corpus Christi

No procession, as would ordinarily be, but at least we had a Holy Hour before Mass, something we don't usually have on Sundays (or Saturdays), so a certain grace.

Wish I could share my faith in the Blessed Sacrament, the core of the Faith, with my Evangelical brothers and sisters by sharing with them the entry from my book today and St. Thomas' writing in the Office. I would that all could know the glory of Jesus' presence, His great gift, here in the Sacrament. It is everything, really.

June 15 – Grandmother

My (Polish) grandmother's birthday. Never met her – she died the day my mom came to bring the news that she was finally pregnant (with me). My birthday is three days from now. I am told she was very religious, and so, likely the cause of my being raised Catholic. Again, never met her but have often heard about her and thank God for her faith, and my own.

Happy Birthday, Babcia!

June 16 – Engendering the Spiritual Life

Dreamt last night of giving a talk while facing a wall, almost alone (coronavirus concerns?)... speaking extemporaneously on the subject of "Engendering the Spiritual Life" (as it turned out). Recall noting the eternal life that is within us and asking how we can recognize it and make it grow. Mentioned, of course, things like prayer and reading and the sacraments; recall getting a modicum of positive reaction from perhaps the only person listening when I said that secular things can also help us, if taken in the right spirit.

Had significant trouble sleeping last night, suffering from neck pain shooting into my shoulders and down my arms, which only seemed to be relieved when I kept my head straight. So I guess the talk could be subtitled, "Getting Your Head on Straight."

June 17 – Medjugorje and Faith

Started reading an autobiographical book by one of the Medjugorje visionaries. Had recently read a couple of nasty critiques of

Medjugorje. Not sure why there is such animosity within the Church toward the visionaries; it seems almost comparable to the anti-religious persecution by the Communists when the visions began. There have been such undeniable fruits from pilgrimages to Medjugorje. Do we not know a tree by its fruits?

I myself had no doubt regarding the visions from the first time I witnessed one on TV in the '80s. All the children's mouths dropped at once when Our Lady appeared to them. And in my three pilgrimages I have been greatly blessed, even miraculously so, though it has never been miracles I have sought. Was never interested in seeing the sun dance but in the edification of my faith, which certainly has occurred in this humble village at the edge of Heaven.

June 18 – 60

Today I officially become an old man, and will remain so till the day I die. Yet I still sense a childlike spirit within me that knows no age. It is this we must cherish always, for it is of the Kingdom of Heaven.

Every day is the Lord's Day, for all life comes from Him.

June 19 – Sacred Heart

Today we hear of the love of God, the love that is God, exemplified in the Sacred Heart of Jesus Christ. And how do we approach that love except by loving others, which we so often fail to do?

Watched a film on BET (on this day commemorating the end of slavery). Here is the heart of humanity, in the black race. Let us pray that heart beats always with love, or what hope has humanity?

June 20 – The Temple

Immaculate Heart of Mary feast... and I but sleep, I but nap. Is it not time to wake? Is it not time to pray? Why should we waste the day given us in Jesus' Name? Why should we fail to become as Mary, the Temple of the Lord, the Father's House where Jesus ever dwells?

This is the day my sister fell.
This is the day for all to rise
(as in the night I did),
to offer our lives, our pain and suffering,
for the salvation of the world.
(It is summertime.)

June 21 – New Life

Ended up reading at Mass (apparently no one scheduled), and discovered while checking the intercessions that the Mass was for my sister. She was in a coma a few days and died on the 23rd, but that date was not available. Had forgotten the day we took instead.

Also Father's Day, which hasn't meant much to me since my dad died eighteen years ago. But the second reading re Adam's sin seemed appropriate since he is the father of all mankind. However, Jesus, the new Adam, is the Father of our new life in the Spirit.

It is that new life I pray my sister and father enjoy today.

June 22 – Offering It Up

Another difficult night. But I seem to be finally learning to offer up suffering for the benefit of others, finding the grace and the light in it. This is something I have read and written about for years, but have not been as inclined to practice.

Have been thinking about/praying especially for my friend who suffers from severe mental illness, and he seems to be doing better of late. But there are so many intentions, so much to be prayed for... I am still not as brave as Thomas More or Bishop Fisher in the face of death or torture, but hopefully am taking a step or two in the direction of the Cross.

In the night weeping enters in,
but with the dawn comes rejoicing
(as we see the fruits of our sacrifice).

June 23 – Lynn

40th anniversary of my sister's death, having fallen from a cliff at the age of 15. We took my mom out to eat, and she watched Mass on TV.

It is something one never really gets over, especially if a mother or a father, or a wayward older brother. But I pray for her today, as I have not done as much in recent years, being complacent and with expectation of her presence in Heaven. But the prayers would at least help me, as they did during my conversion so many years ago, if I remembered more so.

As a child let us be, O Lord.

June 24 – Signs of Hope

I remember waking the morning after the saddest day of my life with the sun filling the room and a certain joy in my heart. For a moment I had forgotten what had happened; it seemed like but a dream.

It wasn't a dream, of course, but perhaps the sense of joy was to reassure me of the state of my sister, that she was blessed to be in Heaven, where there is only joy. This truth I would not come to realize for years, but here was a sign of it.

HOME

She had appeared to my father the night she fell, I learned some time later, reassuring him that she was well. So we both were blessed with signs of hope, signs of what is to come. (I recall this on this feast of the Birth of St. John the Baptist, the great forerunner.)

June 25 – Medjugorje Anniversary

Always found it rather poetic that the visions began a year and a day after my sister's death (messages the following day). That she fell from a hill seems significant as well, since "Medjugorje" means "between mountains".

Reading in Mirjana's book of the persecutions the visionaries went through under the Communist regime should give anyone pause about doubting their veracity. But in the end all that matters is the Faith, which is what will take us home.

June 26 – Miracle Every Day

St. Josemaria's feast day. Realized – upon hearing his essential teaching is to change the world every day, where we are – that the saint's work of God is not dissimilar to the miracle I propose to find every day in this writing (though I often fall short).

It is in the ordinary that the extraordinary may be found, if we have eyes open to the movement of the Lord in our lives.

June 27 – Praying in the Night

For more than ten years I woke every night to pray the Office and the readings for the day. Not long after moving to Florida (almost nine years ago) I began to slack off, getting up later and later in the night, till finally I stopped altogether. It seemed like a necessary thing to do since it was apparent that it was creating a certain tension in me and with my wife – better I tend to my marriage than hold to this ascetic practice. And that seems to have been a wise decision.

But now things appear to have changed and the call I hear is to return to the practice, at least to some extent. Neck and shoulder pain has repeatedly been making it difficult to sleep through the night anyway, and so I often go to the couch not to disturb my wife. I have started praying upon waking in the night, and it has proven fruitful, not only as a blessed sacrifice, a measure of the Cross giving me something to offer up (and reminding me how beautiful it is to wake and pray in the night), but also to give me a certain peace to be able to return to sleep. It was in the past a key to finding purity, and I pray it shall again serve to cleanse the "film of dirt" that covers my heart.

June 28 – Reference Point

Yesterday's entry was confirmed by today's gospel calling us to take up our cross. Waking in the night for prayer is a special cross, one which serves as a kind of reference point for the day. It is a time I feel very close to the Lord, and this sense I repeatedly recall during the day, grounding me in a holiness, a purity... assuring me that I am a disciple of Christ. May it continue, I pray, and inspire a needed conversion.

June 29 – Discernment

Prayed during the night again. I pray it indeed brings a spring of holiness, but must watch that previous problems do not arise and that I am truly following the call of the Lord. It is so difficult to discern at times.

Patience and discernment also continue necessary regarding the Church's reaction to the virus situation and specifically the wearing of masks. Repeated question, problem, of how to be patient with others' fears while remaining clear and reasonable, not to mention faithful. Had been praying for the Lord to end the virus Himself, to show the world that it is He who is in charge and not man. But realized today how I have been imposing my

HOME

own expectations on the Lord. It must be in His time, which I now accept could be weeks, months.... Whatever it is, is up to Him and in His will. And this truth brings peace.

June 30 – The Lord Listens

What if there were someone who knows us and what we want better than we do? This is God, of course, who is love, who loves us, who knows us, and would always do what is best for us... if we let Him.

An example I always think of is Tobit and Sarah, both of whom prayed for death but got what they really wanted instead – Tobit the return of his eyesight and his son, Sarah a blessed marriage. The Lord listens to our heart more than our words.

May we all listen with Him and allow Him to act in our lives. Then we might find true love.

July 1 – St. Junipero Serra

Much tension of late in the country, including the tearing down of statues of St. Junipero Serra (for one) under a presumption of racism, but inspired rather by ignorance or plain anti-Catholic bigotry.

People lack wisdom, discernment, and so are easily deceived and ready to judge. There is an inability to separate the actions of a violent military from the compassionate zeal of the Church regarding the Spanish who came to this country... much less the intelligence to distinguish between good and bad religious and military players.

Serra helped protect and prosper the indigenous population, in addition to bringing them the salvation of Christ (which so many who judge him wrongly have lost or despised). This is simple historical fact. But what is true is not relevant to those who care only about advancing their ideology; and certainly there is no respect for the Faith.

St. Junipero Serra, pray for us.

July 2 – Peace

There was a moment during the (public) recitation of the Rosary after Mass this morning when I ceased my responses and became still, and sought direction from the Lord. And He answered.

Principally He bade me to be at peace, especially with regard to questions surrounding the wearing of masks (now that it is mandatory throughout Sarasota, including outside PP), particularly in church. He did not deny it showed a lack of trust and a lack of respect (toward Him), and left open my sharing that understanding with others, but repeated His call to peace in this whole situation.

I had not had a clear word since Our Lady spoke to me toward the beginning of the crisis, saying it was not as severe as made out to be but that I should show patience and respect for others, and I had been going along with only that as guide. The word today was to reassure my soul and let me know He is with me.

July 3 – Baptismal Day

This is my baptismal day. I can't say we do anything special to celebrate it, though perhaps we should. It is simply not done (despite the past encouragement of at least one priest).

The day we were baptized is more important than the day we were born because our faith is more important than our lives and Heaven is more important than this world (and Baptism is the doorway to the Kingdom).

On this feast of St. Thomas may we learn to appreciate our faith above all else.

July 4 – Patriotic

Can't say it felt much like the 4th of July; mostly forgot it is. The climate in the country and the lack of celebration made it much like any other day. And personally struggling with an anxious mother whose doctor failed to refill her prescription before a holiday weekend has made it worse than a normal day.

But I did take it upon myself to move the American flag in the foyer near the doors leading into the church so all could see it as they enter this weekend. I did it for a person more patriotic than I, but it was my idea... and I felt more patriotic than usual after doing so.

Thinking also of the root of the word "patriotic", which is "father". The Lord tells us we must honor our mother and father, and so one should honor one's country.

July 5 – Crosses and Blessings

The Cross is heavy; the Cross is light. Priest in Confession yesterday asked me to contemplate and embrace the cross the Lord has given me. I could think of several crosses, and each one is both heavy and light – each is a cross, and every cross is also a blessing. I am blessed to still have my mother, though it can be demanding to care for her. I am blessed with my wife, though every relationship has its difficulties. My writing is a blessing, but it is a sword piercing my soul. Every cross is a blessing and every blessing comes with a cross. The key is to carry them with Christ.

July 6 – Bringing Communion

For the first time in over four months brought Communion to the home of my friend who suffers mental illness. Finally received permission to do so. I hadn't realized how much I'd missed seeing him. We just stayed outside his front door a short while talking before the service, but afterward I felt very blessed, a certain joy upon my soul.

July 2020

It was wonderful to get back to this ministry and wonderful to be with perhaps the only friend I have been wont to see regularly.

July 7 – Intercession

During Rosary after early morning Mass, I prayed intently for the Lord's blessing upon the abortion clinic we would soon visit, where counselors were already at work as clients arrived. I prayed for Jesus in the Sacrament exposed upon the altar (in a monstrance containing a Host at least four times the normal size) to hover over the building and for His Spirit to fall upon the square block, converting the abortionist and the staff, enlightening the clients and the counselors.... The prayers were very intense.

And it seems they were effective. When we arrived at Planned Parenthood, one of the early counselors told me that only one client had entered the first hour (while I was praying) and that she was not even allowed in till the end of that hour (as they apparently opened late). Unfortunately, in the hours following the traffic was as busy as usual.

Perhaps, like Moses, I should not have let my arms down. Perhaps someone should be in intentional prayer all the day long. Then maybe we would win the battle.

July 8 – The End of the Virus

Was inspired to offer Stations this morning especially for an end to the virus. As I entered the expansive church, the pastor was praying alone in a front pew. For some reason I felt he was praying for an end to the virus, and I remembered that Christ is present "where two or three are gathered," and so found faith the Lord would answer. I was a few stations in before I recalled that the first reading in the Office this morning was on David's punishment for taking a census of the people – a plague – which he chose because it was in the hands of (a merciful) God, and not man. This reading I have thought much about during this time of pestilence.

HOME

At each station I focused on the intention of ending the virus, and realized the Holy Father could be considered the third gathered, not to mention many others who might have read the Office and made the connection.

May it be so, Lord, we pray.
Let it be as a Christmas gift in July.

July 9 – Age of Perfection

Came to mind today after seeing fruits from my return to waking in the night to pray (practiced in my 40s) and having taken up some exercises (practiced in my 20s) to help my neck and shoulders especially, that senior years can and should be an age of wisdom wherein we take from what is old and what is new to reach the perfection desired all through life. It is not simply God's waiting room; though it is that, too, one must do more than just wait – one must perfect, one must finish, complete the journey, by God's grace, in patience and wisdom. And so, as I see blessed purpose in it, I no longer regret entering old age.

St. Augustine Zhao Rong and the Chinese Martyrs, pray for us.

July 10 – Go

Another day. Brother stopped by. Walked with mom. Late uncle's birthday... This must be the place.

Home.
No place like home.
(Hope you don't mind the poetry.)

Called to press ever forward, always grow in the Lord, never turning back, never becoming complacent. There is no end to life. Go.

July 11 – Fathers

St. Benedict, pray for us. May we all follow your rule of work and prayer, monastic or otherwise. All are called to follow the Lord and balance our lives by His wisdom and grace alive in our hearts and minds. Ears open to obedience may we possess to serve our brothers and sisters.

On this feast of the father of Western monasticism, I pray for two fathers (in tears): my dad's release from Purgatory and a spiritual father's release from pain here on this earth.

July 12 – Prayers

Sometimes my prayers are just words; other times in prayer I seek to surrender entirely to the Lord and His will, hoping to do as He pleases that I might bear fruit in His Name by joining in His sacrifice. But sometimes my prayers are just words. More and more may I surrender to you, Lord, I pray.

(Of special concern of late has been the elderly I see who I know are suffering. My tears are often for them and their consolation in travail.)

July 13 – Tragedy

Birthday of my aunt who recently died.

Was going to write about the priest's sermon regarding Jesus' definition of "peace" and his examples of those who maintained peace even in martyrdom, especially since it reminded me of another priest's word in Confession two days ago, encouraging me to seek peace and wisdom (even in this crisis time)... something the Lord Himself encouraged me to do not long ago.

But I have just received terrible news of the fall of the 22-month-old granddaughter of our principal pro-life counselor, who I have said reminds me of my own sister (who died at 15) with her large,

HOME

innocent eyes. We are told she has a heartbeat but no breath. And so I write this between periods of sobbing, trying to maintain the Lord's peace.

Save her, Lord, I pray. Please.

(And now I read that St. Kateri Tekakwitha, who died at 24 and whose feast we celebrate tomorrow, was beatified the second day my sister lay in a coma. She would die the next day.)

July 14 – There Is Hope

St. Kateri Tekakwitha, pray for us.

Planned Parenthood witness on a day all are occupied with prayer for little Faith. And there are blessings. Faith is now breathing on her own and getting stronger, though we still must pray for the swelling on her brain to reduce. And we have a save.

There is hope. Especially when there is such an outpouring of prayers as today. Never had such reaction from my pro-life email list – everyone and their prayer group is praying. Truly wonderful.

July 15 – St. Bonaventure

St. Bonaventure, pray for us.

Priest said Bonaventure was not only a mystic, but also a good administrator, a rare combination, and I felt a certain affinity with him. Reading again the passage from his *Journey* book in the Office, I was reminded of how well he describes the mystical experience, the speaking of the Divine NAME, especially re "the suspension of the operations of the mind" (the Silence). I remembered I quoted this in one of my books somewhere and thought perhaps I should find it and offer the writing as the basis for a potential talk... but overall I do very little writing of late (only this) and nothing *with* my writing. I suppose there continues some doubt about the purpose of it all, since there has been so little fruit from it, especially during this virus period.

As for Faith, it has been touch and go – getting stronger, breathing on her own... then heart stops and it takes a prayerful miracle to restart it. Stable now but with the swelling on the brain. It is remarkably, and sadly, similar to my sister's fall.

July 16 – Our Lady of Mt. Carmel

Our Lady of Mt. Carmel, pray for us.

On this most beloved feast of Our Lady, little Faith sleeps peacefully, a rainbow outside her hospital window. May she rest in our Mother's arms being healed and nourished for life.

I inquire of the grandparents if the family would consider Baptism in this emergency situation, but they kindly say they trust she is with the Lord.

And I see an elderly friend who has been locked in his assisted living facility close to four months (escaped today to go to church). He said it is like being dead but not being dead. Surely there must be a better, wiser, more humane way to combat the virus.

All the great Carmelite saints, pray for us this day and always. May we be one with you.

July 17 – Lack of Faith

On a day of fasting the Lord gives me remarkable energy to get much accomplished, including finally finishing a letter re lack of faith during this crisis, and getting some proofreading done; and the mother of Faith defends the life of her child against a medical establishment that would quickly end it.

We live in such a culture of death, lacking God, lacking love, lacking faith... and so dwelling only upon fear.

There is hope. Must never relinquish it. Our God is the God of the living.

July 18 – God in Others

Priest said of St. Camillus that he saw Jesus in every person, especially every sick person he tended. (Read this in the Office as well.)

This is something the saints teach us, but something with which I ever struggle, something that escapes me. I suppose it is a lack of love, a lack of God in my heart and mind, but I can't say I see God in others. Though the problem is probably that I don't look for Him there.

And if St. Catherine is right that we show our love for God through our love of others, I fear for my soul. I do love and try to help others... but I can't say I see God in them, except in particularly blessed moments. And that is a problem.

July 19 – Music

Mass was significantly elevated by the music and singing. I realized that a talented singer is one thing, a talented singer with faith quite another. One we appreciate with the mind, but the other raises our spirits unto God. Faith makes all the difference.

This evening my wife and I watched a film about a famous singer who was lost, who was on the run, from himself and from his pain, but in the end found his way home, to his wife, to his daughter, and to himself. We must look ourselves and others in the eye.

July 20 – Playing God

Family of Faith receiving legal and health advocacy as the culture of death closes in on them in the person of a doctor playing God and breathing termination for the child.

Prayers continue.

July 21 – Urgency

Day occupied with pro-life matters. After three hours at Planned Parenthood (and taking mom out for a few hours), got a call from the father of Faith; spent the next three hours searching for a local pro-life doctor and an expert in Catholic end-of-life care. Did much calling and emailing in an urgent effort to help the family avoid the real possibility of removal of life support tomorrow.

Lord, please do not let Faith die betimes.
We trust in you.

July 22 – Life

St. Mary Magdalene, pray for us.

A blessed day as we wake early for Mass and Holy Hour, then drive up to St. Petersburg to witness for the life of Faith outside the children's hospital there, praying and holding signs with forty or fifty others.

And there is blessed news! Even as we arrive we hear that Faith has begun to breathe on her own; and in the end the scheduled assessment (to be used as justification for pulling the plug) is cancelled. And her mother declares what we all always knew – Faith is alive!

Praise you, Lord, for this blessing.
May it be a true turning point on Faith's road to recovery.
We love you, Lord.

July 23 – Exhaustion

I think the Lord works best through us when we are exhausted, when our will is thus broken down along with any walls we build with our minds. Then He can act.

HOME

Exhausted mentally, physically, emotionally after the past couple of days of prayer and work for Faith. Waking this morning, felt as if I'd been through a battle. And I thought of the grandfather, my friend, who was up all night making signs for our witness yesterday. And I remembered in the Bible (and I suppose in war generally) how armies often walk all night and then enter battle the next day without rest. And the Lord blesses them with victory.

Thank God we won this battle by His grace and mercy, and His power. May He make us always ready to serve Him, that the war may soon be won.

July 24 – America

St. Sharbel, pray for us.

Spoke to the Lord about America while praying in the chapel. It is important to bring things to the Lord's attention, not that He isn't aware, but so He knows our heart and we reveal our mind.

I spoke very objectively, saying, "You placed me here in this country...", and this objective look at my life and the Lord's decision I be born here (instead of somewhere else) provided a clear sense of strength and transcendence: I was not tied to this place, as we should not be tied to anything, but I expressed genuine concern for it, and especially for the children growing up in such a confused culture, not even knowing if they are a boy or a girl.

It is up to you, Lord; your will be done.
But what about the children? Help them, I pray.
All is in your hands.

July 25 – Exasperation

St. James, pray for us.

Anger and argument, over what? Nothing and less than nothing. Impatience, frustration... how I lack self-control and the ability to confront a problem wisely and calmly. And on this my name day I am called in Confession to be charitable. How quickly I forget. I had even begged Our Lady in my Rosary so soon before that I might be more like her.

I read today (from a visionary) that every marriage has its arguments, its problems, and I certainly proved that.

Lord, take my exasperation and my exaggeration
and give me patience instead.
Your peace return to my soul.

July 26 – Forward

Sunday, back on point: work toward reconciliation (though forgiveness was already present), Eucharistic visit, reading, exercise, walk with mom... but this evening things seem uncertain again with Faith, especially regarding the hospital.

Sts. Joachim and Anne, watch over her and her family.

July 27 – Blinded

I see how blind we can be, how we see things as we want to see things, according to our own desires, rationalizing error and sin as it suits us.

It is hard to believe how I could still be guilty of such foolishness, and at least a little frightening, for how much more is expected of those who are given much. There is so much the Lord has given me, yet I continue to be blinded so easily.

I can chalk it up to being human, but that does not cover it... nor does it help me avoid the fires of Purgatory.

Help me, Lord, to set my heart on you
and live according to your will and way.

July 28 – Reconciliation

Reconciliation, both with wife and in special Confession. Paul begs us to be reconciled, and how important it is. The Lord's grace can't flow through us if we are not reconciled to Him and with one another. Forgiveness is the name of the game, the Christian life. Without it, without reconciliation, we tempt the fires, if not of Hell, at least of Purgatory, which is something we should most want to avoid. (This has been my principal prayer for a long time.)

O Lord, have mercy on my soul.
Keep me close to you.

July 29 – Hospitality

St. Martha, pray for us.

"We are travelers on a journey without yet a fixed abode; we are on our way, not yet in our native land."

The quote is by St. Augustine from the Office for St. Martha, who so often welcomed the Lord Jesus into her home and fed and cared for Him. And He took respite there. Such is the virtue of hospitality, so much treasured by Jewish culture, and many others.

But Augustine's point is that, as good and as necessary as it is to be given a roof over our heads and food on the table, such gracious blessing is but temporary, for as Christians we do not find our home here in this world but in the Kingdom of Heaven. It is the Lord who prepares a room and sets the table for us in *His* House. Praise God!

July 30 – Proper Care

After our witness a week ago and then another prayerful gathering the other day, and mostly owing to Faith's beginning to breathe more so and more strongly on her own, it does seem the hospital is now moving forward with proper care, especially nutrition (which had been lacking at least a couple of weeks) and so the worst has indeed been avoided. The prayer is that this care continues well and the little one continues to improve. May she be in the Lord's hands and come by His grace to full recovery. (God be with her and her family.)

July 31 – Watching Sports

Modified baseball season began last week. Been watching the Mets. Some heartbreaking losses already, including tonight (after they led by six runs). Such a challenge to know how to approach sports – to cut it out completely, take it with a grain of salt, or what. I know I can get overly involved and probably wouldn't be watching, except for some reason I find myself getting the games down here on a sports cable station. What does the Lord wish to teach me? Hope to find an answer soon. (And the hockey playoffs start next week.)

St. Ignatius, pray for us. Help me to discern.

August 1 – To Wait

Waited an hour on line for Confession – hadn't done that since pilgrimage to Medjugorje. After Mass there were about eight people on line so I went into the chapel to pray a Rosary (Confessions are in a room off the hallway rather than the confessional in the chapel, due to the virus situation). When I came out twenty minutes later, there were eleven people on line! It was a new priest (and first Saturday), so more people went, and he took much time with each (like Medjugorje). After an hour there were still a few people ahead of me. Was relieved to see our parish priest, who peeled a few of us off the line.

I guess it would be difficult to wait an hour in any situation. It was hard to stand so long (sat on the floor after a while), and it didn't help not being with Jesus in the chapel... nor that I've been taught Confession shouldn't take more than 2-3 minutes. But I think the thing that tested my patience most was not being prepared for the wait. (Had things to do and Confession usually doesn't take much time at all.)

It made me think about Purgatory and what a principal problem may be for those who find themselves there: it would be especially hard if one did not expect to go there and was unprepared to suffer long.

I suppose the lesson is – be ready to wait, ready to suffer. Do not presume on the mercy of God or on your own virtue. This is true for our tasks on earth, but especially our life after death.

August 2 – Singular Focus

I keep praying, intermittently, to find a singular focus on being a Christian disciple and so following the voice of the Lord. I seem to approach it at times, but it still hasn't rung in my ears or sunk into my heart. I could abandon myself to the will of the Lord, but can't say I know what that is. Even re individual questions I am not clear.... Perhaps this is due to a failure to seek sincerely, to ask Him directly, and to trust in His presence, that He will answer. (Or perhaps I do not want an answer.)

I pray in waves it shall come to me in fullness eventually.
O Lord, let my heart open to your call.

August 3 – Identity

Subject of identity theft. Someone used my info (and many others') to apply for unemployment benefits, for me, in Colorado! Received the debit card a couple of days ago; on phone today addressing the problem.

Thought about the word "identity". I am not my social security number, and it was that which was stolen (along with date of birth, etc.) and not my identity. I know it is the "official" identity which is meant, but still, people can forget who they really are and get lost in these official records.

Who are you? A primary question we all must answer. Let us find our identity in Christ, and as St. John Vianney (whose feast we celebrate tomorrow) encourages us, direct our hearts to where our treasure is, in Heaven.

August 4 – Hand-Washing

Jesus' declaration that it is not what enters the mouth but what comes out of it that corrupts the soul could not better summarize the problems with the reaction to the current virus – it is the spiritual that matters more than the physical. The priest notes that the hand-washing rituals the Jews performed were to prevent disease, but seemed unaware that the saying provides chastisement toward those (like himself, since he has persistently preached mask-wearing) who are so concerned with avoiding germs, but show little trust and faith in the providence of the Lord.

It is a good idea to wash one's hands, but it is a better idea, and most necessary, to put things in God's hands.

August 5 – Terrible Combination

Came to terms with the struggles I have gone through in my life regarding sexual sin: a terrible combination of a heart wanting to help others, with a weakness that makes it easy to confuse such care with sex. Experience of pornography at an early age likely made the weakness deep-seated and, so, difficult to overcome this side of Heaven. But knowing one's problem is the first, and major, step to conquering it and preventing further problems... with prayer.

(Terrible chemical explosion in Lebanon, bringing destruction to half of Beirut. Prayers are with our Maronite brothers and sisters.)

August 6 – Transfiguration

I pray to the Lord for the purging of my sins, the purification of my heart, fully realizing it is only by His grace we can change and become a new creation. And as I stand before the Lord in the monstrance at the end of my face time, the Host shines with a golden radiance.... Perhaps He shall answer my pleas and I shall be transfigured. He has the power. I am willing.

August 7 – What I Wish

Couldn't go to the far side of the adoration chapel (furthest away from others, so I can let my mask down) since someone had taken my place, so I sat on the opposite side, near Our Lady. Was drawn to her despite Jesus being on the altar. Prayed for a pure heart, a cleansing of all the perversion and pollution within me.

Mary responded that the Lord would purify my heart if that is what I wished. So the question became, is this what I really wish? (It would be His will.) So I then had to pray for it to be my wish, my genuine desire, whatever sacrifice, whatever cross might come.

And St. John of the Cross speaks so well in the Office of union with God, of sharing in His glorious divinity. This is what I wish, O Lord!

August 8 – Strafing

St. Dominic, pray for us.

A rather torturous day as trials and temptations assail me and I come close to falling into sin. Like an internal strafing was the pain necessary to endure. But all is well as I pray and prostrate myself before the Lord, and confess my sins. And in a later reception of Communion I realize the grief of the delay and how the Sacrament brings union with God.

We should always remember how the devil works to bring us down just as we resolve to draw closer to the Lord.

August 9 – Silent Voice

Lectored at (Sunday) Mass. The first reading was of Elijah on Mt. Horeb, waiting for the Lord to reveal Himself. The prophet knows him not in the wind or the earthquake or the fire, but in a still, small voice.

I thought to speak quietly and take my time with the words "tiny whispering sound," and then pause, letting the LORD speak His NAME (YHWH) in the silence. I have long believed this is what must have been done when the Word of God was read aloud and the speaker came to the Divine NAME – he must have been silent. The NAME was lost likely due to impatience with such a pregnant pause... and so the LORD's presence with it.

We need to rediscover the NAME of the LORD even as we need to rediscover the silence in which He speaks. (I hope what I did today was a help.)

August 10 – Roses and Lilies

Suffering some emotional distress that has me on the verge of tears... not able to function normally or go along with usual routine this evening. Think I must talk with someone to resolve certain issues. Sent an email to a priest friend.

St. Lawrence suffered a terrible martyrdom but did so with great faith, and so no fear. St. Augustine tells us there are all sorts of flowers (roses and lilies...), all sorts of calls to lay down our lives. May we each find our own.

August 11 – Hope

Before going to Planned Parenthood, prayed intently during Holy Hour that there would be "not one of these little ones lost," not one. And I believed the Lord could do it. Prayed the same during our hour of prayer at the site, very intensely, and still I believed it could be – even if the Lord had to turn back the clock. (And I still believe it.) And we were blessed with at least one save, and a couple of referrals.

I prayed also a new culture of life would go out from this moment, from this place, to the ends of the earth. And I believed it. The Lord can do anything.

And we pray for little Faith today as she suffers from a condition for which she was not getting sufficient medication. And I can't help but compare Faith's situation – as I am told it will take time for her to recover, to heal – with watching one of the longest games in NHL history, won finally by the team Faith's family (and I) root for ardently. They had the most shots in history and finally got one in the net in the fifth sudden death overtime period – after seven and a half periods of hockey, equivalent to two and a half games, more than six hours of play.

There is hope. Be patient.

(And I wear for the first time today (at PP) a T-shirt on which I ironed the letters H-O-P-E.)

August 12 – Marked

A certain peace today after a good rest last night... though prayer not very deep until I kneel in front of the Lord on the altar before leaving the chapel, reaching out to Him to realize His presence and why He would come among men, and how He could accomplish it – the crucifix provided the answer.

O Lord, may our foreheads be marked with your Tau,
that we might be protected by you
at the end of the age.

August 13 - Blind

Devastated by my selfishness, my ignorance, my foolishness, and how deep it can go, and how blind I can be.... This has happened to me a number of times in my life (though not like today), and still I do not learn. It is as if I have been a greater sinner in the last fifteen years than ever before. It makes me fear for the future and what will be my next mistake, the next sin of which I will be unaware until it is too late.

May God help me (and us all).

August 14 - Josephite Marriage

St. Maximilian Kolbe, pray for us.

The Lord seems to put a call on my heart to a Josephite marriage. It might seem sudden, but was actually present at the very beginning of our relationship: my first proposal was for such a marriage, after spending thirty days with marriage as the question, going through a personal Ignatian retreat using his book. And it has come up a few times along the way.

But now the call seems to be whole, sincere, and life-giving, a fulfillment of our marriage and spiritual life. (And the readings for the day spoke throughout of marriage... and forgoing it for the sake of the Kingdom.) Though I doubt my ability to do it, I find trust in the Lord's grace. May it truly be in His hands.

August 15 - The Assumption

Mary was assumed into Heaven, carried by the angels to the Lord's side, where she intercedes to bring us where she is. O to be like Our Lady!

Heaven is our goal. Heaven is our home. We must find our way there on the coattails of the Blessed Virgin, who precedes us all to our Heavenly home.

HOME

Returned to the chapel for the first time for (Saturday morning) Mass. A step home. I pray we are coming gradually out from under the shadow of this virus into the light of day and back to full lives in the Lord.

Into your hands, dear Lord, through Mary our Mother.

August 16 – On Hands and Knees

The Canaanite woman comes to the Lord on her hands and knees, as we all should, as is just. And justice has its rewards, even as truth does not exist without love; for Jesus loves the woman, as He loves us all, but all must know the truth that we are but dogs before our mighty God – our love could never compare with His, for our arms could never stretch so wide to reach those so far below. But His can, for He is the only One so far above us all.

I seek self-control, realizing finally how much I need it, how much I lack it. I pray I come on my hands and knees to beg it of the Lord, that He might have mercy on my poor soul and I might live in His love. May I have the same blessed faith of the Canaanite woman and find my place at His feet.

August 17 – Awaiting Acceptance

The gospel of the rich young man asked to sell all his possessions seemed a confirmation of the call to enter a Josephite marriage, to give up what I might desire most (like Ezekiel in our first reading, whose wife was taken from him by the Lord) in order to draw closer to God.

But the call awaits acceptance, or it cannot be said to be true. I continue to pray the Lord's will be done, and with blessed decisiveness.

August 18 – Ask What You Will

Spoke yesterday with mother of mentally ill friend about their situation regarding the potential fix-up of their house by the city. Would take at least a month, including a week on the bathroom. They are thinking my friend (who sleeps most of the time) would have to go to a hotel, and maybe her too.

After Communion this morning I knelt in a profound silence and remained for a while after others had stood to pray; then after the final blessing the (retired) priest announced he had to try to rent out a mobile home he bought but hasn't been able to move into. It may not work out – no furniture in the place as well as other hurdles – but when he said it, it seemed an answered prayer, somewhere my friend could go for a month or so and not have to pay for a hotel. Had been praying for a few intentions (including this one), remembering Jesus' exhortation to ask for what we will and He will provide.

August 19 – Peace in the Storm

Very dark, ominous morning as I head out early for Mass to peals of thunder and black clouds, which had an otherworldly glow (not far from sunrise). As Mass began, a torrential rain started to pour down upon the roof, making it difficult to hear the first reading, wherein Ezekiel spoke of great woe. It quieted some as the priest began his homily, and he noted that it was like the silence in which the Lord speaks after the wind and the earthquake pass (a reference to Elijah on Mount Horeb).

But it wasn't until after I received Communion that this silence, this peace in the midst of any storm, came upon me in a profound way. And I realized how right St. John Eudes is about our being the breath and heartbeat of Jesus, and that this is truly accomplished in our reception of His Body and Blood. No thunder could disturb this union.

August 20 – Fruitful

St. Bernard, pray for us.

A day of work, and prayer. Up early and continual action throughout the day, getting things done. It is such a grace to be productive in the Lord, to be fruitful as we human beings were made to be. May sloth be far from me; may I be alive in the Lord's will. May my prayer always be, "Thy will be done," for in this is every prayer, is our blessed alignment with the will of God, whose will is always done. Amen.

August 21 – From Utter Darkness

In the night I prayed, then sitting in a dark room I realized I could see nothing, absolutely *nothing*, however much I tried. For one who has always lived in a city with streetlights, nightlights, etc., this just never happens. (The only comparable experience I can think of was in the Smoky Mountains when the sun went down and I couldn't see my hand in front of my face.) The window and door were blocked just right to make no light visible.

At first I found real blessing in the experience, even said I could see better than I ever have (spiritually). But soon a fear came upon me as I realized I really couldn't see a thing and wondered what I'd do if permanently in such a state. It was like Peter walking on water, then sinking upon noticing the wind and the waves.

I believe the Lord was trying to teach me how blind and how utterly dependent upon Him I am. And I suppose the fear was part of this lesson.... But not long afterward, problems with my wife were resolved by a blessed conversation, and I was not alone.

Tonight we watch a drama on Jonah, who spent three days and three nights in the dark belly of a whale but was thrust out onto the shore. And in today's first reading Ezekiel calls the dry bones to arise.

August 22 – Queenship of Mary

Priest tells first Communicants at Mass this morning that Jesus is King of kings and Mary is His Queen Mother who intercedes for us at His side. And on my knees before her, as I pray my Rosary, I beg that my consecration to her be sincere, be more than just words, that I might truly serve the Lord. I beg, yes, I beg all the emptiness be taken away that to her side I might come and dwell where she is, with Jesus in Heaven. O let these not be just words!

August 23 – Extolling the Cross

It is a Sunday so St. Rose of Lima's feast day is not celebrated, but every year I am challenged by her words in the Office of Readings extolling the need to embrace the Cross, to treasure it for the glory it brings. Since I am apt to complain at the slightest difficulty, I am easily convicted of my failure to appreciate, much less desire, the Cross.

I pray there is hope for me still. But even my prayers are so often empty. I try today to realize this and apply myself better to prayer, to the words I read in the Liturgy of the Hours and the mysteries on which I meditate in the Rosary.... And though in the Mass I find a certain union with the Lord, so much progress needs to be made to obtain proper gratitude for the gifts the Lord provides and not waste the graces, especially of the sacraments.

My mentally ill friend, who suffers so much, witnessed to me today that he offers up his pain as much he can. It is understandable how he might fall short. But what excuse have I?

August 24 – No Guile

An Israelite with no guile in him. Such is Nathanael/Bartholomew, from the Lord's own mouth. A remarkable thing to say; a blessed thing to be. The goal of us all: to be a genuine follower of the Truth, of the Christ. To set our heart completely on service of God.

This is as we all should be – focused on the Lord, living for Him. I see that today, and I see how I do not do it. Faith in the Christ, knowledge of His presence among us, and love for Him, should overwhelm us and set us on a path directly to God. But how far short I fall.

So many distractions there are, so many excuses... so much guile with which to contend. How shall we be as this child? How shall we be a true disciple of Jesus, and see the angels ascending and descending upon Him? Open our eyes, dear Lord, our eyes and our heart. And let us follow you, who are the Christ, the Son of God. What else is there?

August 25 – Discouragement

So hot in Florida – mid-90s every day and terrible humidity. Three hours at Planned Parenthood not easy to endure, but the Lord provides a breeze and the strength. Still, there is discouragement and a lack of faith. Discouragement because I pray so hard, so intently all morning for conversion and turnarounds... but no saves come. Not even much positive interaction. And at the same time I lack the "hope" I have written on my chest (though not on my heart). And so I don't really *expect* the Lord's intervention, and become distracted from the goal and desire to go. At the same time I fail to focus, I also fail to place it in the Lord's hands... and so I am doubly to blame. But it is so hard not to become discouraged, and so hard to remember what is going on in our midst.

Lord, please bring life to all souls.

(We must love our enemies,
forgive and pray for everyone's salvation...
join the Lord on the Cross.
Only then.)

August 26 – The Smell of Abortion

The virus has been significantly decreasing the last couple of weeks, particularly here in Florida and in our area. But of course there is little mention of this in the news, though when it was on the increase the first five minutes of every cast was filled with negative details and profiles.

Abby Johnson spoke at the Republican National Convention last night. A most remarkable speech, something that would have been unheard of in the past. As a former Planned Parenthood director and witness to abortion, she provided graphic detail of its horror, including its smell. I pray that smell rises to the nostrils of all who promote this abominable practice, especially the politicians and the media, that this "virus" will get its proper coverage.

August 27 – Call to Life

St. Monica, pray for us. May our tears join your own for all our brothers and sisters, all our children and grandchildren, all our neighbors and friends, and all our enemies who remain outside the arms of the Church, the Mother of all God's children. Thank you for your prayers and for your son, who is a light to us all, calling us so clearly to eternal life in our Savior, Jesus Christ.

I find the Lord hearing my own prayers, for my marriage, for an end to the China virus, for life (there was a save yesterday after all!), for Faith and for my depressed friend. May finding such answer increase my faith more so to pray the Lord's will be done on this earth and in this country.

Donald Trump accepts nomination toward re-election (as I write). It has indeed been remarkable to see the issue of life so prominent at the convention, not only with Abby Johnson, but also a Catholic sister who spoke so well; abortion was on the lips of so many speakers. How different from the past, when a bare mention, a crust of bread, was the most we could hope for. It is now in the light. May all see and be convicted.

August 28 – His Presence in Others

Praying for people as they pass by on their return from Communion. Kneeling in my pew I can see Jesus in each of them, as He is quite literally at this time. I say I struggle to see Jesus in others, but it became clear to me today as I realized this obvious fact.

Why don't I always notice this? Why is this not obvious every day at Communion time? I think it is because I just don't recognize how marvelous this moment is, being too familiar with the reception of Christ. (I also ordinarily have my head down as I pray after Communion, and usually sit closer to the center aisle, where people approach the altar.)

O let us realize the grace and blessing we have in receiving Jesus and being among others who share such blessing! Let us not take Him and one another for granted but remember and see Him present. Open my eyes, Lord, to your presence in others, especially my brothers and sisters with whom I attend Mass each day.

St. Augustine, pray for us.

August 29 – The Blessing of Confession

Thank God for the sacrament of Confession; His mercy truly endures forever, making us new, however "old" (in sin) we had become. Every week I experience this. After penance, praying the Rosary kneeling before Our Lady and then the Lord, I am able to surrender openly to the will of God, ready to serve Him alone... ready to die to self and live anew.

Thank God for the sacrament of Confession, and the power of prayer to unite us to the Lord.

August 30 – Marriage Blessing

Something of a miracle occurred in my marriage this morning, something that shows our marriage is real, that it is maturing, that our love is able to withstand difficulties... that the devil will not get the best of us.

I praise God for my wife and my marriage. May He stay with us always.

August 31 – Sister's Ring

Lost my sister's ring last week. Hasn't turned up. It had been on my pinky (just past first bone) for thirty-four years. Put it on a few years after her death – never took it off. People always said I'd lose it, but I wore it showering, swimming, sleeping, washing my hands... it was very secure behind that first bone. But I've been losing weight lately and that must have been the cause.

I pray that if the ring doesn't return to my finger, my sister will be more so in my heart.

September 1 – Upsetting People

I seem to have a knack for upsetting people with my words, especially via email. People repeatedly take things I write the wrong way, a way not intended... and it creates problems not easily fixed. The more I try to explain, the worse things seem to get. At the moment my brother is angry with me, which hasn't really happened in years (can't remember when, beyond our adolescence). And there are certainly others who have been offended as well. I simply don't know how to correct others. Should probably leave well enough alone much more.

September 2 – Others First

Came to a clearer realization of the anger and selfishness that is so much a part of my character as I treat my wife with kindness and patience, deferring to her and giving her the attention and respect she deserves. I understood her vulnerability and had a clearer sense of what it means to put the other before oneself (something the priest also spoke about).

We were at the Luncheon for Life for the first time in several months and it provided opportunity to become aware of my interaction with her and others (haven't been out much of late). I just wish I could maintain such a proper Christian attitude, but am afraid of my forgetfulness. May the Lord help me to remember and Our Lady pray for me to find the personal conversion she speaks of again in her message this month. I realize, too, how it is only by God's grace I can become a better person, and hope that I am correct in thinking that He may be doing this work in me at this time. (O to become a truly spiritual person – this was my thought and prayer as my wife and I prayed the outdoor Stations together.)

September 3 – Intentional Prayer

Reconciled with brother, both of us apologizing. Answer to intense prayer. Praise God.

Prayed intently for Faith, too, and sent a package (a Lightning cap celebrating their first Cup) to her grandfather, my friend. Also ordered a book on Heaven for my (inquisitive) mother... and drafted a pro-life sign for the parish, asking people at adoration chapel to pray for the babies on abortion day, to support us in our work.

St. Gregory the Great, pray for us,
for all the Church...
for healing and strength.

September 2020

September 4 – Diet and Exercise

Have been losing weight recently, so much so am a little shy about fasting today (Friday). To start the day my weight was below where it usually is *after* a full Friday fast... as low as it has been since Holy Week, when it ordinarily reaches its lowest point. I suppose it is because I have been eating less and exercising more since a yearly checkup showed my cholesterol climbing again. That report has proven to be a blessing because I have found better health the last couple of months. And in the process the Lord has also answered another prayer by healing pain I had been experiencing.

The Lord provides what we need and the means to what we need.

September 5 – Overcoming the Darkness

Outdoor Stations in the morning heat, no shade; Mass following for deceased Knights; then Confession with priest who hadn't slept well....

Mother Teresa, pray for us,
that the darkness we may overcome
by the Light of Christ.

September 6 – Intercede for Others

A blessed Rosary with the Knights online. Joined the meeting a minute late, forgoing lunch (after being delayed by an extended Eucharistic visit and having helped out after Mass...), but we seemed to harmonize immediately with the person leading. I felt a certain gravity that tuned me in to the Rosary right away, and it lasted throughout the prayer. Very pleased we decided to wait to eat.

As lector, I read aloud Ezekiel's call to be a watchman and warn the wicked; then when I read Paul's declaration that love is the fulfillment of the law, I enunciated each of the four examples of the commandments he listed. The commandments are love.

Also, tried to pray for everyone again today at Communion time, and in general as well. For others we must intercede.

September 7 – Closer to Christ

Labor Day so only one (earlier) morning Mass. Arrived an hour before but the church was not open so I prayed the Stations outside (where it was actually a little cool). I then went to the window I hadn't visited in a while to look upon the tabernacle and pray till the sacristan came.

Once inside, I prayed in the chapel, looking more directly upon the tabernacle, and I realized the gradual difference between the two views. Then I imagined again being *inside* the tabernacle with Jesus, and how I had forgotten His call to be His tabernacle.

After Mass in church I returned to the chapel to pray and, having received Communion, realized the next closer step – Jesus was now inside me and I was indeed His tabernacle. I considered how long this state might last, how long Jesus would be physically present within me... and I remembered that we become what we eat: the food becomes part of our bodies. And so in this real way we become the Body of Christ, which is the goal – to have Jesus live in me and I live no more. But I fear my forgetfulness. (Though perhaps He remains with us even as we leave His presence and get lost in the things of the day. Would that it were so.)

September 8 – Mama Mary's Birthday

It seemed for a good part of the day radical prayers for no abortions at Planned Parenthood were being realized as traffic was unusually light in the morning and it actually appeared it could be no clients were there for abortion. Unfortunately, that changed rather quickly in the afternoon, as traffic picked up and abortion-minded women became more obvious. It felt as if my prayers were only half-faithful, as if they couldn't be sustained (though it was wonderful as long as it lasted).

O Mother, help us fulfill our faith in the Lord and His power to do all things, even to bring a new culture of life to our little corner and around the world. May this be our present from you, and to you.

September 9 – Chastity

Gifted with a transcendent sense of purity this morning, reminiscent of the early days of my conversion. The first reading today extolls virginity, but I was forgetful of this when praying and receiving the gift. I had read the readings in the night and somehow did not make the connection. My forgetfulness became clearer when I was asked to sub as lector an hour before Mass. I didn't have a chance to check the readings, and simply couldn't recall what they were, despite still being in that pure state.

But Paul also says the married should remain married, and our marriage is blessed today. Any chastity for me must be in the married state. May it be so, Lord, I pray.

September 10 – Truth *and* Love

On a day Jesus tells us in the gospel to love our enemies, I get a video from a friend of a priest breathing condemnation upon the Democratic party and mocking straying clergy. But I also watched a civil debate between the leaders of Catholics for the two presidential nominees.

Focusing on truth does not excuse us from showing love. We must have both truth *and* love, we must speak the truth *in* love, or we have nothing, or we are not Christian, failing to emulate Christ on the Cross. Even David in the OT understood the respect due those in authority, refusing to harm Saul even as the king hunted him down for no reason but his own jealousy. How much more should we?

We are living in days where everyone follows what he thinks is right, essentially becoming his own pope and king; obedience is now the greatest sin.

September 11 – Politics

Back and forth with friend(s) via email re the video mentioned above. I am just very concerned that politics is taking precedence over the Gospel. I have certainly been praying the current president, who has been particularly and unabashedly pro-life, will be re-elected, especially since the alternative is extremely pro-abortion (and other things); but hearing religious people – who think virtually the same as I and with whose politics I generally agree – become unkind, mocking, condemnatory... makes me wonder and even tends to put me off the vote I am quite sure of.

Pride is a terrible sin, the worst there is, and it overrides any good we might do. I pray humility for all.

September 12 – Mary's Communion

Read today that Mary had a renewal of her intimate union with the Lord, known at the Annunciation, with every Communion. But it seems to me the reception of Communion would not be necessary for her, as her union with the Lord was never broken or lagging. Isn't this what Jesus taught when He asked: "Did you not know that I must be in my Father's House?" in answer to her fear of losing Him. *She* is the Father's House, His Tabernacle, and He is *always* with her. We need to return repeatedly to the altar to receive our Lord anew; I do not see that she did. I don't know, of course, but I don't think she ever partook of Communion, simply because it was not needed. He is always with her. (This is so physically even, as we have learned that cells of her children remain in the mother's body.)

Had a sense of union with the Lord this morning, an ascetic transcendence encouraged by my fast yesterday (under 150 pounds for first time in years) and a lack of sleep, and increased by the blessing of Communion and Confession, not to mention Stations and Mass and prayer service (for the unborn). O to be as She is, one with the Lord!

September 13 – Weakness

A weakness followed yesterday's sense of transcendence, perhaps from the same source – lack of food and sleep, ascetic practice. It was like the sour stomach that followed the sweet honey of the scroll in the mouth of the prophet Ezekiel. It could have been the word I offered my two friends, which had given me peace, turning... as one person cut off communication and I feared the other might too (though that conversation later ended in mutual understanding). Or it could have just shown the difficulty in discerning what is wise and good, and what is detrimental in the spiritual life. Maybe I went too far. It is a fine line to walk, I suppose.

September 14 – Triumph of the Cross

A blessing to make it to Mass and Holy Hour, despite some continued stomach upset, tiredness.... My prayer is always that the Lord will enable me to make it to church every day (for the rest of my life). This is indeed the greatest blessing.

And Scott Hahn spoke well tonight of the blessing of the Eucharist, as well as the Cross, tying the two together. He echoed what I realized some time ago and is celebrated in today's feast – the Cross is the greatest gift. The greatest suffering, the greatest tragedy (the crucifixion of Christ) is the greatest blessing, the source of our salvation. And it is His glorious presence we receive each day in the holy sacrifice of the Mass.

September 15 – Our Lady of Sorrows

Finished book by Medjugorje visionary, and one of the last things she mentions is just how painful it is to see the sadness of the Blessed Mother, which is magnified, as it were, a billion times our own (perhaps for each sinner in the world). And the priest in his homily this morning echoes the same, that because of her Immaculate Heart she feels sin more acutely than we sinners for

HOME

whom it is blunted. And how she cares for all, how she would lead all away from sin to her Son. O let us turn from sin!

And today is abortion day at Planned Parenthood, where the sorrow is overwhelming, where the Mother of God must watch mothers enter to have their own children killed.

But the sorrow, all sorrows, can be transformed into joy by the power of the Lord (as priest leading Zoom novena says), if we but turn to Him.

September 16 – Love

First reading from I Corinthians 13. How essential is love, true love, the love that is God, that lays down its life for others like Jesus on the Cross. It must be who we are. And yet, as I read each of Paul's descriptive words, I find myself so much the opposite: impatient, unkind, rude. I pray there has been improvement... but still there is so far to go (and how I desire to avoid the fires of Purgatory!).

I can say that the Lord seems to be blessing my marriage of late; prayers to St. Joseph appear to be answered, and for this I do thank the great Patriarch. I pray this will be a means to finding the love we all must have.

September 17 – When Faith Fails

Went to another church for Mass since ours was to have only a Communion service. The door was still locked when I arrived (about a half hour before Mass), so I went over to the office to inquire when adoration might return to the parish. To my pleasant surprise the Sacrament was exposed in the small chapel next to the office. I asked about it, but quite foolishly did not stay to pray my Rosary there, instead going back over to the church as planned, somewhat afraid I might not get a seat in this small church with severe seating restrictions. Of course, there were very few people present all the way up to Mass time... and I ended up experiencing the warring prayers of one elderly woman who recites the Rosary aloud every day (mostly alone) and another down the pew from her who decided to pray her prayers aloud. It was a real cacophony.

O what troubles we find when not led by faith! I am supposed to be so desirous of adoration, and yet I left Jesus with barely a thought. And still I had time to return when I realized what I'd done, but did not. How much fear and a lack of faith remain with me. How much I need to come on my knees before the Lord like the woman in our gospel today, washing His feet with my tears. O how tears come to my eyes when I hear Him say, "Your faith has saved you; go in peace." O that He would say it to me, and I would take it to heart.

September 18 – In the Lord's Hands

Regaining health, strength, the past few days. After feeling faint while kneeling and praying at Planned Parenthood, perspiring greatly, I took some water and later, while becoming more active (and sweating even more so), felt sickness disappearing. Gradually getting strength back. Didn't do a full fast today (Friday), but kept to it generally, and it seemed to help my return to health as well. Also exercised rather vigorously despite fasting, and there, too, found strength.

Our lives are in the Lord's hands and it is never easy to predict what will or will not benefit us. Can't go simply by physical or material factors. Sometimes that which seems it should be detrimental – like a fast when weak – is just what we need, if indeed put in the Lord's hands.

September 19 – Viva la Virgen!

Our Lady of Penafrancia Fiesta – devotion of my wife's region in the Philippines (of which I am an honorary member). We've been taking part in the nightly Zoom novena leading up to today. (The Association is in NJ, but the virus gave us a chance to participate from Florida.) Praying especially for Faith's recovery.

HOME

When we were dating and first married, the fiesta celebration was very large – in Liberty State Park with over a thousand people. More recently it has been in a local park with a few hundred. They also ordinarily have a fluvial procession (i.e. in boats). Quite an event. Bless the devotions of the Filipinos. Wonderful to have faith so much a part of the culture.

Our Lady of Penafrancia, pray for us!

(And on this fiesta day, Sylvia found my sister's ring.)

September 20 – For Him

Helped out cleaning church after Mass, then Eucharistic visit to a friend, quick lunch, and Rosary with Knights online. Good to be doing for the Lord. Not a burden, a blessing.

The last line of today's gospel answers well how the first will be last: "Are you envious because I am generous?" Do we envy the grace showered upon others by the Lord? Do we expect Him only to favor us? And, especially for those among us who have spent many years serving the Lord – do we expect special treatment in return? Then we are not doing it for the love of God and are not really with Him. We do not treasure the great gift of being able to work for the Lord.

May all be blessed, from the greatest to the least! May all know the glory of union with Him, in our work here and in Heaven.

September 21 – Scapular Anniversary

St Matthew, pray for us.

It was nineteen years ago this day I had blessed and put on for the first time my Trinity scapular. It was just ten days after 9/11 (the smoke over the City was still visible from my back window). For a few weeks I had been making the scapular from a piece of silver bought in NYC and using tools lent to me by a jeweler friend. I have worn it every day since.

September 2020

Today Jesus says to Matthew, "Follow me," and these words strike me as I thank the Lord for all the many gifts He has given me, and beg Him that I might truly do His work. I seek to realize how I might be falling short, and I see that efforts along usual ascetic paths have not brought progress. So it seems it is in the everyday miracles I must find my way.

And the Lord provided a special blessing this anniversary day – during my face time with Him, there was no glare on the glass before the Host in the monstrance. This has never happened before (or since). I am always having to move to one side or the other to be able to see Jesus without hindrance, but today I saw Him clearly wherever I knelt or stood or stepped. Quite remarkable. I believe it was indeed a special blessing from the Lord.

Also today, Sylvia received a beautiful reliquary from her good friend; it contains relics of three great saints: Francis, Benedict, and Padre Pio. Another wonderful blessing.

O Lord, by your grace may I follow you more so each day.

September 22 – Faith

Grandparents of Faith, our veteran pro-life witnesses, came by Planned Parenthood today. It was wonderful to see them but heart-wrenching to hear the story of Faith's accident. However, in addition to toe wiggles, she also recently breathed above the respirator (for an hour) for the first time since a trach was put in several weeks ago. These are very good signs. And they've found a pulmonologist to help them.

So many are praying for little Faith, whose second birthday was yesterday. And souls are being drawn closer to God through all of this. It is astounding to see how the Lord can take great tragedy and turn it into a blessing (as He did on the Cross) – He will always triumph over the devil's wiles.

September 23 - Hope Never Fails

Padre Pio, pray for us.

Kickoff rally for 40 Days for Life, Shawn Carney speaking. A blessed moment for several reasons, but especially for his recounting of St. Maximilian Kolbe maintaining his faith in the darkest place on earth and inspiring others that hope never fails... even as we stand in the lot of our little pregnancy clinic, in the shadow of Planned Parenthood's monolith directly in front of us. Evil will not prevail.

And there is much talk about (and interviews done on site by a pro-abortion TV station) a potential Supreme Court nominee, as she is blasted for her devout Catholic faith.

September 24 - Seeking Chastisement

Learning to ask intentionally for chastisement that will bring purification, or at least accepting it when it comes. Asked for it two days ago, and at Planned Parenthood found it with a man who threw the brochure I offered him to the ground. I realized I had to pray for him if I were to be a true Christian (even as I held the crucifix during our prayer time). I did pray for him, and tried to take his pain and anger upon myself.... Was also subject (with others) to the berating of another angry man defending abortion - him I needed to correct/chastise. And, as mentioned, listening to the stories about Faith from her grandparents (who found her in the pool) was indeed heart-wrenching as well, and brought tears.

Today I accepted chastisement for poor treatment of my wife and for the aggravation I experienced at a dental office regarding charges and services. I pray I shall be able to continue asking for and accepting the crosses the Lord provides.

Thank you, Lord, for you are just and merciful, and express your mercy in your justice, and your justice in your mercy.

September 25 – He Provides

Syl's birthday! I thank God for her and wish I could celebrate with her more so.... May the Lord help me appreciate this great gift.

Sold stocks that I had switched to my name. Will give the money to my mom but take the taxable income on myself, to make the ACA minimum. How the Lord takes care and blesses us. It is truly remarkable how He provides.

September 26 – Florida Home

Thirty years ago today my parents closed on this house and moved in. Nine years ago today my wife and I arrived to take up residence in Florida. Tonight the Tampa Bay Lightning play to win the Stanley Cup, and I am rooting for them here in our new home state. But the fact that this is the first year we have not returned to NJ for a months-long stay makes it seem more so that this is becoming our permanent home. (May not be able to leave for any length of time ongoing, because of my mom.) We managed to get through the heat of the summer without much trouble, another significant sign. Perhaps we are here to stay.

September 27 – The Spirit on the Waters

Have been thinking for a while about writing on the moment of Creation, and got potential first words today: "It was dark, very dark. Pitch dark. There was no light at all." I don't know if I will go forward with writing a book or an essay or anything... but this moment is of absolute significance and has been in my thoughts for many years – at least since coming to an understanding of the Divine NAME – and is particularly significant in my own acts of creation, especially conceiving new titles.

I have on the wall beside me a photograph of a newly ordained priest praying over Sylvia and I. In that moment I experienced a most profound sense, or vision, of the wind moving upon the waters, of the Silence from which all words speak, from which all Life comes. This is the source of prophecy.

September 28 – Where Do I Live?

Poor sleep and a dream in which I could not remember where I lived. Was in NJ and went to our first apartment; when I rang the bell a black teen came down the stairs, not my wife. I proceeded to try to help him with a pronunciation question.... I then remembered the last apartment we lived in before moving, thinking maybe that is where I live. It wasn't until I heard a noise and began to wake that I realized I live in Florida now.

The most disturbing part of the dream was sensing I was experiencing some kind of dementia (though in teaching the boy my mind was clear – thought it might be a call to return to teaching). Then during the day felt tired and a little sick, and even did things like dispensing cold water through my teabag and not realizing it till I sat down to drink. (Never done that before.)

O Lord, take my mind.

September 29 – Sports and Balance

Sports has ended for me for a few months at least – Mets season ended a couple of days ago and the Lightning won the Cup last night (finally). But the question of how to relate to the games remains. I wrote many years ago about the need to keep the game in the background as it transpires, and this holds some good insight (not to get too involved or let the ball play you), but a kind of Buddhistic Nirvana is not the answer because we are a sacramental Church that needs to engage in a real fashion with the people and things in our lives. We must go through the flesh to get to the Spirit because we are human beings, not angels. And so there must be a balance between a healthy transcendence (to keep things in perspective) and a healthy engagement (to remain genuine, real... humble).

Sts. Michael, Gabriel, and Raphael,
pray for us poor humans
racing in this stadium.

September 30 – An End to Abortion

Worn out, tired, sick, causing me to shorten my Holy Hour, nap, and snap at my wife and mom. Probably due in part to late nights watching hockey playoffs recently, as well as standing outside in the heat at Planned Parenthood, and then again at a Rosary rally.

But did pray a rather intense prayer kneeling before the Lord prior to leaving the chapel – prayed for the Church to be a beacon of light to bring life back to this country and the world, and I sensed the Lord heard me and would answer my prayer for an utter end to abortion and its support. May He make its horrors evident to all by the means He chooses.

O Lord, let your will be done.

October 1 – Till the End

Thinking, praying, and talking with my wife about what we, especially she (since I am likely to go first), might do if/when the other of us dies. We have no children (and my only brother has no children of his own), but my wife does have a couple of nieces with whom she is close, and still a couple of sisters in the U.S. I wonder if she would stay in Sarasota anyway if she were very involved with the parish, perhaps as sacristan.

But the main thing is to entrust both the rest of our lives on earth and, most importantly, our lives after death, to the Lord. This is my prayer. He has watched over me (and us) many years and so there is no reason to think He will not do so till the end. We must but set our sights on Heaven.

O Lord, I am longing to labor for you,
labor that will bring me to your Kingdom.
Peace be unto this house.

HOME

St. Thérèse, pray for us.

October 2 – Guardian Angels

May they watch over us and guide us on our way
home to Heaven.

Amen.

October 3 – Only in Heaven

While emphasizing that we should "rejoice that our names are written in Heaven" and not in the things of this earth, however marvelous, the priest specifically says that we are on a pilgrimage journey to our home in Heaven, and so should not get distracted even by great spiritual blessings like those the disciples revel in today.

O let us set our sights on the Kingdom
and rejoice only in the King's presence.

October 4 – Speak

Was moved to write to grandparents of Faith, again asking why not Baptism. They had said they entrusted her to Jesus, but it occurred to me this is just what Christians do via Baptism, the universal sign of such dedication. Also mentioned a few Scripture passages, including those supporting infant Baptism.... Praise God, they are very understanding, so I suppose my fears about bringing it up again were unwarranted – had hesitated to speak until I read warning against silent shepherds in the Office this early morning.

Also, priest gave a good homily for Respect Life Sunday (and we had an hour of adoration before Mass). We must speak and do as called by the Lord without fear of reprisal, though always with love, and respect.

October 2020

October 5 – The Fullness

Mentioned yesterday to a young man looking to enter the Catholic Church that, yes, other churches can be blessed with great music and preaching, etc., but without the Sacrament, the fullness is missing; I would say the *essence* is missing. And it dawned on me today that what is missing is love itself, and to be more specific, God Himself. Remembering what I wrote here recently after listening to Scott Hahn correlate the sacrifice on the Cross – the greatest act of love – with the Blessed Sacrament, the Eucharist, I realized just how at Mass this love becomes present in our Communion with the Lord and His sacrifice. Without that, what have we? And I realized decades ago after going with a friend to Times Square Church following Sunday morning Mass at my humble parish, that even though there was two hours of tremendous preaching and music and praise at the NYC church, and people could barely understand our pastor's homily (and the music was pedestrian)... still in that "weak" forty-five minutes more occurred simply because of the Sacrament, of Holy Communion. There is no replacing it. There is no substitute for God Himself being present.

October 6 – Seek Truth

I've noticed repeatedly how difficult it really is to get to the truth in any matter. There is so much supposition and hearsay (and ignorance), and so little effort to seek the truth, that one wonders if there is much of any news one can trust. I notice this especially when I am directly involved. I first witnessed it decades ago when I had to submit a summary of our Little League games to the local paper. Invariably they got the facts wrong, and very wrong, even though written down in black and white.

Today at Planned Parenthood I was told by a few people there had been a save. But I discovered, after tracking down those most directly involved, that there wasn't a save, and certainly not today. A young woman who'd had an appointment at the pregnancy center a few weeks ago came back today for an ultrasound with members of her family. We were just thanked by the mother for our presence on the sidewalk.

And today the 40 Days for Life national email said that Saturday at our PP - a day that has been closed for business for a few months - had been an abortion day, which it never was. (I can speak most authoritatively on this since my wife and I had been there on Saturdays for years.)

So, what news can you trust? I think the point is that we must always be searching diligently for the truth, always seeking what is, and we will find the Lord, and He will lead us to all truth. We must not simply listen for what we want to hear or, worse yet, construct a reality of our own making - something tragically common in society today, seen particularly in justification of abortion and invention of one's gender.

There is a genuine reality and we must seek it and live it.

October 7 - No Trial

Our Lady of the Rosary, Our Lady of Victories, pray for us.

The election cycle nears its end (vice-presidential debate in the background as I write). I pray the Lord's will be done, that a victory in His Name be won through Our Lady's intercession. I pray His mercy on this country, that we need not be subject to the trial, that somehow, some way, Life will return to these shores, to the world.

Today Jesus teaches the Our Father to His disciples. It ends (and I am moved when I hear), "Subject us not to the trial." How I desire to avoid that final trial. And I pray this country and this world may avoid such a trial.

Mama Mary, do pray for us!

October 8 - Falling

Didn't cope very well with a series of difficulties, from dental problems to car problems to banking problems... all coming one after the other. The Lord has watched over me so well that I am not used to having such worldly difficulties. Guess I am a little spoiled. But these are the crosses, and if I don't learn to bear them and bear them well, what good will I be? Must keep going back to the Lord and remembering who I am. May He forgive me my many failings.

He is merciful, indeed, and ready to forgive and reconcile with us; but there is a line between accepting His mercy and presuming upon it, between His lifting us up when we fall and our negligence in falling.

October 9 – God Knows

Ironic that second reading in Office was about development of doctrine, making me think of John Henry Newman (who is famous for expounding upon this), and then at Mass the priest announced that this is, for the first time, Newman's feast day, which I didn't know. Very coincidental – or Godincidental, as it were.

Then my brother stopped over for the first time in a month and we spoke a while about the Beatles and especially Lennon's songs... without remembering it was his birthday (which I did know).

As the priest noted (quoting Newman), we don't always know what is happening in our lives, but God knows what He is doing.

Do as you will, O Lord.

October 10 – Adoration

For the first time since we left NJ nearly a year ago, I was able to experience adoration every day of the week. Our parish ordinarily has it only Mon. – Fri. (other parishes also only weekdays), but throughout October the pastor has allowed it between Masses for an hour on Sunday morning; and today (Sat.) because of a Rosary rally held in our parking lot, the Sacrament was exposed after morning Mass and throughout the rally.

HOME

I could feel it, feel its fullness. Hadn't noticed the lack till I experienced it continually this week. How I wish it could be available every day all the time so I need never miss a day. Praise you, Lord, for your presence among us. Come closer to us.

Also remembered my idea for a House of Prayer in the city with perpetual adoration. First time in over ten years I strongly considered proposing it again. Thought it might be practical to approach the bishop since we have money saved up for a home, and we could purchase according to his wishes. Also thought the reliquary we recently received would be a special blessing for a chapel.

October 11 – Home

Running, dancing, on the elliptical machine listening to a song that begins with the word "Home". Inspired especially by the lyrics, "Never for money, always for love," and "I come home, she lifted up her wings / I guess that this must be the place," I raise my arms and think of the angels, and Lynn, and Sylvia... and Jesus. And I am ready to leave this world and go to Heaven even as I hear, "And you're standing here beside me / I love the passing of time." I am ready to enter the Light.

October 12 – Waking

It has been threatened of late, but still can say, Happy Columbus Day.

The Lord has been waking me before dawn every day for the past week or two, and I have been rising to pray the Office of Readings (at least). I thought He was taking this practice from me again, but it returns rather gracefully, His gentle touch upon my waking. And it has not seemed to disturb my wife's rest. So perhaps this ascetic practice does still hold spiritual benefit for me. Certainly prayer is better focused in the night, and it helps my concentration, my turning to the Lord, in general. So if it is His will, I pray it continue. Amen.

October 13 – Inspired Externals

Deacon notes in his homily that it is not that externals are bad (Jesus confronts a Pharisee in the gospel); the question is whether or not the heart is complicit.

I thought about all the practices I have adopted over the years surrounding Mass – prayers before, during, and after, as well as hand positions, additional signs of the cross, etc. I think it is good that these (and other spiritual "externals", like the scapular, liturgical shirt color, rosary at hip...) have indeed developed gradually over time, each being inspired *from within*. The multiple signs of the cross began before but were greatly encouraged by participation in a Ukrainian Catholic Mass; when I first wore a shirt of the liturgical color of the day, I felt the arms of the saint (Stephen) around me.... Each has had a particular inspiration from the Lord.

I praise God for them because my ability to focus on the Mass has been sharpened so much now that I have in a sense "perfected" my participation; and the other externals have likewise helped to express and fulfill my commitment to the Lord and His Church. So I thank Him that they have grown in this organic fashion, from the heart, and not been imposed arbitrarily.

October 14 – The Spirit Speaks

Supreme Court nominee faces a couple of full days of grilling from members of the judicial committee, answering their questions without notes. At one point she is asked what she has in front of her and holds up a blank note pad provided by the Senate. It is evident to me she is relying on the Holy Spirit, doing as Jesus instructed His disciples to do when led before tribunals. It is He who speaks for her. (The fact she is a member of a Charismatic community serves to substantiate this observation.)

And this is why she impresses everyone with her intelligence, humility, honesty and integrity – these gifts come from the Spirit. I pray many will see in her the true face of Christianity. She is a great witness, and should certainly give example of what it means to be a fair, objective jurist, and so perhaps change the horribly divisive political climate in this country. (The members of the committee were noticeably more civil in her presence.)

October 15 – Contraception

Sylvia and I were at Planned Parenthood on a non-abortion day for the first time since April (when they closed Saturdays), as coordinators for 40 Days for Life for our parish, and so had the opportunity again to hand out literature on birth control. Sylvia gave a brochure away as soon as we arrived, and I spoke for a short while with a woman who had discovered the problems with contraception and was reversing course – she welcomed the literature and I encouraged her to look into NFP.

I have long realized that artificial contraception is at the heart of the culture of death, the gateway drug leading directly to abortion by training women (usually beginning as teens) to adopt the "My Body, My Choice" mantra, to take even matters of life and death into their own hands. It serves well the abortion industry, not only by encouraging this mindset, but also setting the women up for the perceived need for abortion when the contraception inevitably fails. (A lucrative business model.)

But today I discovered, in reading about the Supreme Court hearings, that contraception is at the *legal* heart of the culture of death as well. Both the pro-life nominee and her pro-abortion inquisitor drew a direct line from the decision that made contraception legal (Griswold v. Connecticut) to Roe v. Wade, which of course made abortion legal... and to Obergefell v. Hodges, which legalized same-sex marriage. How I pray at least those who claim to be pro-life will come to see the diabolical significance of the contraceptive mindset and practice so pervasive throughout society. There is little hope of finding a culture of life otherwise.

October 16 – Jesus

I used to know Jesus so intimately; I could speak with Him always. But now it seems only remotely do I remember Him, do I consecrate my life to Him. I do this in the morning, and I have done it permanently... but in the moment, day to day, I neglect to offer Him my prayers and actions. I try today. I try, and when I unite what I am doing with His sacrifice, He is there. He is there as He once was, as I pray He shall ever be.

O my Lord, help me to remember you,
to offer you more consciously
and more conscientiously
all the things of my day.
Be near, Lord, and let me be near you,
my Jesus, my Savior.

(Also today when I proclaimed at Mass the psalm verse, "On the ten-stringed lyre chant His praises," I thought of the ten albums of *Songs for Children of Light* and wondered about their production (or lack thereof).)

October 17 – Trust in the Spirit

Today's gospel was the one referred to a few days ago with respect to the Supreme Court nominee's responding to committee questions without notes. This trust in the Holy Spirit has been the foundation of my writing for a few decades, especially notable, I suppose, in *Our Daily Bread*. I do not map out beforehand what I will say (or revise after), but get an idea, an inspiration (perhaps a title) and just write, trusting in the Lord. Of course, knowledge of the subject and of the rules of grammar is necessary, but faith is the key ingredient.

I also practice this in conversations, particularly those that challenge the faith or present other difficulties. It is the Spirit's guidance we must always rely upon, and it has never failed me. It comes in accord with my faith.

Do not fear, and do not trust in your own intelligence or power – the light of God alone gives wisdom and strength.

October 18 – Political Persecution

Priest gave an inspired homily on Jesus' word, "Give to Caesar what belongs to Caesar, and to God what belongs to God," using St. Thomas More as a prime example – particularly in his moving declaration before his beheading: "I die the king's good servant, but God's first." The priest spoke clearly of how we must always keep God first, accepting whatever persecution may come because of our loyalty.

He also spoke of the current Supreme Court nominee as a contemporary witness of how one can serve one's country and be obedient to its (just) laws, yet keep the Lord and His call first. Our true witness to our Catholic faith will bring society the light it so badly needs, regarding humility and service, truth and love.... (As I have mentioned before, she has already begun to do this.)

I had tears when he repeated More's dying words, but also when I realized who was at Mass today, when because of the continuing virus situation the Sunday obligation remains suspended – it is the more devout Catholics, those who take the faith seriously and so appreciate the fact that, though it may not get as bad as Elizabethan England, we could indeed be persecuted for our faith here (particularly if one party returns to power in the upcoming election). I believe this is why people clapped after the homily.

I pray again the Lord will have mercy on us
and on this land,
which, as with all things, is in His hand.

October 19 – Houses

Impossible to get rid of timeshare without paying the company a significant sum to take it – seems as inescapable as hell.

Sylvia and I watch a show called *Fixer Upper*, wherein a Christian couple does a wonderful job of remodeling homes in Texas inexpensively. We keep saying we'll move there and let them work on our house, though in jest.

Still haven't mentioned to Sylvia that thoughts of a House of Prayer returned to my mind.... Meant to today, but it didn't happen. Perhaps we'll simply stay where we are.

October 20 – Too Much Blood

One of those days at Planned Parenthood when one just wants to give up, watching client after client pour into the death mill with barely a glance at those standing at the gates praying and offering assistance, offering hope. One accomplice drove out crying; another walked away in shame... but most are steeled for their mission. O Lord, help us! (It is indeed a time to put all in God's hands, and to remain faithful, if not successful.)

St. Paul of the Cross (patron of my childhood parish), pray for us! There is too much blood.

October 21 – Offer It Up

Pain. Lack of sleep. Try to offer it up.

Have always been unable to sleep much on my right side because of sinus problems and a rotator cuff tear; never been able to sleep on my front, and very little on my back. Last night unable to sleep on my left side because of shoulder pain that comes only when I lie down on it – as if it's being crushed. Only able to rest in a recliner, though sleep is very intermittent.

So hard to trace the source of pain: too little exercise, too much, the wrong kind.... Three nights in a row with poor sleep, getting progressively worse, so hope I can find some kind of solution.

But it is something to offer up, and there is much to offer it up for. (We did early voting today, which points to one thing.)

October 22 – The Lord's Accomplishments

Pope St. John Paul II, pray for us!
The great Pontiff's feast day.

I was struck by the first reading, where Paul says the Lord is able to accomplish far more than we could ask or imagine, for He provides a decent night's sleep when I thought it impossible. All is really in His hands, especially those things we cannot put our finger on. It is the finger of the Holy Spirit that must indicate our path. May He guide us in all things through the intercession of JPII.

Sleep was likely helped by a full fast (bread and water only throughout the day till the next morning) for the first time in weeks, if not months. But there again it was He who gave me the ability to complete the rather severe fast without difficulty, hardly noticing I was doing it. (And once again, as I have often experienced, I woke feeling particularly strong, my legs like two trees.)

October 23 – Unity

Today Paul speaks of the unity to be found in the Body of Christ. Our witness at Planned Parenthood has been a prime witness of that unity. But there have been one or two people who are jeopardizing that unity and witness, and it has become apparent to virtually everyone. Several of us have spoken with the parties, to no avail. So the rather unprecedented, though very Biblical, move of speaking to their pastor is now planned.

But even as there is commiseration over such disunity and unchristian witness, we hear of a save that resulted from the loving witness of a few of our counselors three days ago - an abortion pill reversal. This is the fruit of love and unity.

I had also prayed for the common good, especially considering the upcoming election, during my Stations this morning. Specifically, I thought about the coming generations, the children. I have to admit this is not something I consider as much as someone might who has children or grandchildren. It reflected a sincerity that went beyond my own concerns and so was a particular blessing.

It is to be like Christ to think of others before ourselves, to pray for what is best for all. In this is freedom. And I thus put the country and the election in Mary's hands, trusting that whatever happens is for the best, and find peace (especially after anxiety of previous night's debate).

October 24 – Act of Kindness

Had a good experience with a store worker today. After dropping my wife off at a house where she was to pick up the pilgrim statue of Our Lady of Fatima, I drove to a natural foods store to pick up some steel cut oats. (I didn't want to go into the house for the final prayers since the woman wasn't expecting me and I wasn't sure how she'd feel about a stranger in her home in these virus days.)

I couldn't find the oats so I looked for the bulk manager. I was helped by a guy who said all they would trust him to do was take out the garbage (told him I would trust him with much more); then when the manager told me they had no bulk oats in stock, he recognized my disappointment and did me the favor of giving me some prepackaged oats for the bulk price (less than half). Now that was an act of kindness, a good turn for a needy customer.

But the biggest blessing today was gaining approval from pastor to have a Holy Hour after morning Mass on Saturdays.

October 25 – Crawling Home

Never did like the Tampa baseball team (Rays), but since I am getting acclimated to Florida, and they are in the World Series and are a rather endearing team – no apparent stars, everyone working together as one, seemingly very humbly – I have found myself rooting for them.

HOME

Last night (though I wasn't awake for it) the game ended with an odd play, featuring two errors and a stumble. The Rays were down one with two out and men on first and second. The batter looped a single to the outfield, and in his rush to throw home, the outfielder dropped the ball. So not only did the tying run score, but the second runner broke for the plate as well. However, rounding third and heading home he stumbled and fell to the ground, and it seemed he would be out easily. But the catcher hadn't noticed the fall, and so, trying to rush the tag, he missed the ball... and the winning run came crawling home. The most memorable moment was the Rays player lying flat on his face, his hands stretched out and tapping home plate repeatedly. He made it.

(And it looks like the home football team will also do well this season.)

October 26 – God's Schedule

Had hoped to get dental appointment this week (before insurance period ends) for a crown and two fillings, but the receptionist said they were all booked up, especially today, since everyone had confirmed. I asked her to let me know of any cancellations. Not long after, she called and said the 9 a.m. just canceled, could I get there immediately? That wasn't really possible, so I apologized and asked her to continue to keep me in mind. Less than half an hour later she called back to say *another* patient had canceled and they had plenty of open time. So I went over and got my crown done. (Side note: dentists always say I am a great patient, not requiring anesthesia even for a crown. I unite the pain with Jesus on the Cross, and remember it is for my good.)

A blessed side effect of my sudden change in schedule was that I had to go elsewhere for Mass and had the priest who speaks quite simply (and even has a bit of a speech impediment) but whose words for some reason carry great meaning for me. (He spoke, for instance, of the woman bent over for eighteen years healed by Jesus as now being able to worship God erect with hands held aloft, as is Jewish practice.) The Spirit of truth (and love) must really be in him.

October 2020

And this evening Amy Coney Barrett was sworn in as a Supreme Court Justice. May the Lord bless her and her family.

October 27 – Disappointment

Terrible disappointment today. Spoke several minutes with a woman going into Planned Parenthood and, with help from others, convinced her to go over to the pregnancy clinic with one of our Spanish-speaking counselors. It looked like we had a save. Unfortunately, she did not go inside the pregnancy clinic, perhaps knowing she would keep her baby if she saw her ultrasound. She ended up in PP for three hours. Just remarkably sad to lose a life so close to being saved. God help us!

It was particularly disappointing on this the birthday of a cousin's son who was born out of wedlock and who served as inspiration for the cover image of *Songs for Children of Light* – a baby in the fetal position, conceived at the time of his birth. It was painted over a water stain on a ceiling panel and became a present for my cousin's son at his christening.

October 28 – Ghost Town

Sts. Simon and Jude, pray for us.

This is the anniversary of the death of my Polish grandmother and the feast of a saint popular with so many Catholics from my hometown: St. Jude, patron of impossible causes.

Fr. Groeschel used to joke, "Why is everyone in NYC so depressed? The light at the end of the tunnel (Path train) is Jersey City." My mother didn't appreciate her beloved city joked about with derogation, but there always was a certain poverty, a kind of despondency, like a dark cloud, over the city. However, as my mother's attitude shows, that did not prevent its people from loving it and finding joy therein, particularly the joy of family and faith.

Now it is a different place – due to tremendous gentrification – so the sense and the joke are not so appropriate anymore. This could

HOME

be seen as St. Jude hearing our prayers for mercy... or as a loss of identity. Even twenty-five years ago I wrote a poem titled "Ghost Town," lamenting the lack of children in the old neighborhood. May it be so populated again.

(Watched a film this evening wherein the lead character was seeking her way home. Home is where the heart is, yes, but it is also where family is... and most of all, God.)

October 29 – Four Corners of the Universe

Two and a half hours sweating in the afternoon sun (still 90 and humid) back at Planned Parenthood. Out all day.

Four Corners of the Universe returns to mind as I read in the Office (Wisdom) of how the Lord organizes the universe, and consider the questions surrounding racism of late, as well as a couple of articles read yesterday.

It seems to me we can neither put people in boxes nor say we are all the same. We must recognize our differences and see how we are all put together by God as one body – heart, mind, soul, and strength: the Black Man of the South, the Yellow Man of the East, the Red Man of the West, and the White Man of the North. Each has his particular God-given characteristics.

These are but the corners, and in a real sense no one lives in a corner. But certainly the differences can be observed and discerned that we might understand one another's strengths, as well as one another's weaknesses, which come as a result of sin, of failing to fulfill our gifts as the Lord ordains.

(It might be wise for me to seek to share these thoughts and writings on the Four Corners to fulfill my own call.)

October 30 – Christian Love

Paul's letter to the Philippians is such a loving one. When I read at Mass, I tried to remember the kindness he exhibited and reflect the intimacy he felt toward the Christians at Philippi. I think it was effective. I looked up at one point and saw by her expression at least one woman had been touched.

O Lord, touch us all with your love,
which flows through your apostles.

October 31 – Detachment

Woke this morning with a wonderful sense of detachment from the world, ready to leave all things behind; like "the deer that thirsts for running streams," the Lord was all I cared about. But though, as with Paul, I would have preferred death and being with Christ, I realized it is better I stay here for those who need me, in particular my wife, and better prepare both myself and matters that still need tending to.

It was wonderful to know this transcendence, though; I pray it stay with me and soon remain always. Praise God.

November 1 – All Saints Day

The first antiphon of Morning Prayer read, "The saints found their home in the Kingdom of Heaven," and our journey home became the theme for this day on which we celebrate and call upon all the saints in Heaven (where we hope to be, praise God).

As we enter November, I become aware that this writing nears its end. I conceived it to begin and end on Nov. 9, the feast of the Dedication of St. John Lateran, the Pope's Cathedral and so the cornerstone church of the Faith. Only eight days remaining. Not sure how it will end, especially with the election upcoming, but I pray it brings me closer to the Kingdom. All the saints in Heaven, pray for us.

November 2 - The Poor Souls

Praying for the poor souls in Purgatory has been a foundational element of my prayer life for twenty years. Each day I do an average of four acts sufficient to gain plenary indulgence - Stations, Rosary, Bible reading... and virtually all in a chapel or church, so adoration is always part of the practice as well.

The Church allows only one plenary indulgence per day, but I petitioned Pope Benedict XVI more than a decade ago for dispensation allowing me to gain additional indulgences for the poor souls. I didn't receive response, but in praying about it I realized that, even if no such dispensation were given, it might still be possible to gain the additional plenary indulgences; for if they were not plenary, they would be partial, and it is possible that the partial indulgence associated with the act could be enough to bring a soul to Heaven - thus partial would become plenary in its application.

At this time I sincerely miss visiting the graves of my father and sister and other relatives and friends, all of whom are buried in New Jersey. I would go to the cemetery every week up north, and at least twice during this novena week, when there are special indulgences (which the Pope has made available to the end of the month this year). Unfortunately, cemeteries, especially Catholic ones, are very lacking here in Florida. Most Catholics are cremated and their ashes poured into the ground on church property... without a marker. I find that sad.

Eternal rest grant unto them, O Lord,
and let perpetual light shine upon them.
May the souls of all the faithful departed
through the mercy of God rest in peace. Amen.

November 3 - Day of Hope

A day of hope, and of prayer.

Filled with hope this morning, and throughout the day, after praying intently for purification and offering all intentions of the day to the Lord. And there were some important intentions today... for the election, for a friend's daughter undergoing biopsy, for the babies at Planned Parenthood – and all the prayers were, as I say, filled with hope.

We had at least one save and a few referrals at PP, it seems my friend's daughter may be OK... and we are hopeful about the election. It was wonderful to be filled with the Spirit of God and trust in His providence, no matter what.

Lord, have mercy on us.

November 4 – Election Days...

In the gospel the Lord calls us to take up our cross and renounce our possessions; and before Mass I look up at the crucifix above the altar (a quite remarkable one of some kind of transparent wire) and I see Jesus dead. It is almost frightening how He sags, lifeless, nothing left. It scares me in particular because, though when we went to sleep last night there was every indication the pro-life, pro-religious freedom, pro-family candidate (the current president) was well on his way to victory, early this morning everything changed – those states wherein he seemed to have a comfortable lead slipped away.

Some are claiming corruption at the polls. I don't know. At the Luncheon for Life one of our leaders said, "Sometimes God hits the pause button" to encourage us to pray more. This was precisely my thought. We must keep that hope alive despite any darkness. Our preferred candidate may still win, or he may lose. But even losing may be a blessing if it causes subsequent elections to turn in our favor. We must give it to the Lord.

What I am called to do is pray. And I do this during the day – entering into the silence of the LORD, emptying myself and calling for His truth, His light to shine through... as it inevitably will. We must keep our sights on this light that never fades.

November 5 – The Poor Pharisee

It seemed it might be a brighter day, but then I heard that my friend's teenage daughter has lymphoma... and the difficulties with the election continue.

Listening to the gospel wherein Jesus speaks of the rejoicing in Heaven over one repentant sinner, I realize He could be speaking (is speaking) about anyone, everyone, and in particular about the Pharisee standing before Him. Not only he, but we too, must realize he is as great a sinner as the ones obvious to all at table. And Jesus calls all, desires the repentance of all, and chastises all to produce such repentance, for He loves all. And I get a tear in my eye when I sympathize, with Christ, with the poor Pharisee.

And I pray today for that Pharisee, for whoever in power might be corrupt, particularly as I continue to pray for truth and light, the light of Christ, to shine upon this country and this election.

November 6 – Citizens of Heaven

I know we have our "citizenship in Heaven" and am very grateful to Paul for that reminder today, but it is still difficult not to fall into depression over a troubled world.

It looks like this writing will end (in three days) on a very dark note. And I wonder if it will be my last published book as I recall the first, also a kind of journal (though poetry), which ended on 9/11... The two would make appropriate bookends.

As one presidential candidate is about to claim victory, the other prepares lawsuits claiming fraud. If the fraud is there, that is most disturbing; if not, we will have a president and a party that will bring significant persecution to those of us who are pro-life, pro-religious freedom, pro-family.

The diagnosis of my friend's daughter also has me very sad. We will go and pray over her tomorrow, and hopefully discover charismatic gifts the priest encouraged everyone to investigate today. In addition, little Faith remains in a coma; and I haven't heard from my depressed friend, who has been sleeping for three weeks. And the number of COVID cases is increasing, though the severity seems less.

If that is not enough, the report on the disgraced cardinal of my former diocese is finally set to come out next week. It portends to show massive corruption in the Church in America.

It is almost a weight too heavy to bear, but suffering does purify the soul, and so for this we should be thankful. It hopefully reminds us we are indeed citizens of Heaven.

November 7 – Revival

On this day I wake with the still, small voice of the LORD speaking in my soul, and experience a kind of revival.

We prayed over my friend's daughter with her family, and will bring a spiritual director to her tomorrow. She looked good and seems a strong young woman. I also got a text from my depressed friend in the middle of the night (as if he'd read my entry yesterday), and saw an interview with an intelligent and sincere poll challenger who spoke of considerable (and alarming) corruption he witnessed in Michigan, which appears to have been repeated in other states and makes it seem possible the candidate the media is declaring victorious may not be.

What occurs to me in all these situations is that it will take a long time for each of them to be resolved, and so patience is the primary need. "Death must be active within us if life is to be active within us," as St. Ambrose states in the Office. Death kills sin and leads to resurrection. (May we all be like a long distance runner, as is my friend's daughter.)

We also had Saturday morning Holy Hour for the first time today, another blessing and reason for hope.

November 8 – The Fall

If the darkness and difficulties were not significant enough, it hit closer to home as my 92-year-old mom fell this morning and broke her hip. She had an operation which we are told went well (I stayed in the hospital praying for a couple of hours during the surgery, *Fixer Upper* on TV above my head), but this will certainly be a new chapter – I pray a long one – as we care for her. She will need around the clock care for some time, and may require at least a walker after that.

My wife and I managed to duck out for Mass in the early evening, after hearing of the operation's success, and rushed back just before the end of visiting hours. Got to her room, wished her good night and blessed her, though she was still very much knocked out. (All this on what would have been Sylvia's mom's 99th birthday.)

November 9 – Zeal for the Father's House

On a stormy day when schools are closed and adoration suspended, and I am a bit overwhelmed regarding problems with my mom's condition and the limited hospital visitation due to the virus, I find myself very exhausted as I write the last entry of this book on the Dedication of St. John Lateran, the cornerstone church of Christianity.

It is the day I proposed to Sylvia, the day we inaugurated the adoration chapel in Jersey City, the day on which the Church itself is recognized and celebrated... the Church we all are as temples of the Holy Spirit, the Church Sylvia and I live for in the love of God.

Two years ago on the three days following this one, I wrote *A Plan of Life for Children of Light*, the principal quote of which is, "Zeal for the Father's House consumes me," as it does Jesus in today's gospel. I pray that zeal continues and finds fulfillment in the Kingdom.

O Lord, I give this holy day to you.

Postscript

January 6, 2021 – Light in the Darkness

As I prepare this manuscript for publication, a final word.

This is the traditional date for celebration of Epiphany. The Lord makes Himself manifest. A Light shines.

But it is mostly a day of darkness, for the country and the world. Today the pro-life party unexpectedly lost two Senate runoffs (including one to a pro-abortion "Christian" pastor), and so now the other party holds complete power in the federal government. I noted the darkness of the day to a friend as we left morning Mass, and he said we are being punished for all the abortions.... As he said that, I came directly upon the baby Jesus on the floor in front of me – there He is, in every child.

The darkness notwithstanding, there is light that has come: my friend's daughter has been diagnosed without cancer; and though there were dark days for a few weeks, my mom is now on the mend and gaining strength after her fall. Faith remains in a coma, but she has been doing better of late, as has my depressed friend. The China virus is yet with us, but I still do not know anyone personally who has gotten it here in Florida.

Finally, Congress was to certify the electoral votes today; however, they were delayed several hours when after a peaceful rally the Capitol was overrun by some of the president's supporters, who believe their concerns about fraud have not been adequately addressed. What shall happen next, who can say?

It seems the only mercy the Lord has left is indeed punishment and persecution. How we need the Light of God, the Light of Truth to dawn in our midst!

O Lord, help your children of light
shine in the darkness.

OTHER BOOKS by JAMES KURT

"TURN and Become like Children":
Refuting the Presumed Contradictions of the Jerusalem Bible
Old Testament Commentary –
A case study recounting the problems afflicting modern biblical scholarship as exemplified in the JB.   188 pp.   2019.

"Into Your Hands...":
Distillation of the Letters of Fr. Jean-Pierre de Caussade –
Reflections of the profound counsel of Fr. De Caussade to embrace the Cross and find the Lord's will (and joy) even in our greatest sufferings.   82 pp.   2019.

Prayers to the Saints (Updated) –
A page of prayer to each saint on the General Roman Calendar for the United States.   237 pp.   2019 (original 2007).   w/ imprimatur.

Our Daily Bread:
Exposition of the Readings of Catholic Mass –
A page of writing for every Mass of the liturgical calendar for the Roman Rite; reflections drawn from the readings.   727 pp.   2004.   w/ imprimatur.
Our Daily Bread: Lent – 86 pp.   2019.   w/ imprimatur.

Remembrance of Things Present –
A mystical work seeking the presence of the LORD in the moment, where He dwells at all times.   100 pp.   2018.   w/ imprimatur.

Two Books: Paradox and the Christian Faith /
     Hippie Convert –
The apparent contradictions of the Faith are explained for those who seek wisdom; and a member of the flower generation addresses true love and peace, in poetic form.   238 pp.   2016 (reprinted 2019).   w/imprimatur.

Lines of Grace: Meditations on Verses of Holy Scripture,
The Stations of the Cross, and The Most Holy Rosary –
A Catholic devotional especially for the encouragement of the practice of plenary indulgence.   195 pp.   2016.

Christian Vision of the Old Testament –
Synopsis and exhortation; faith-filled overview of all books of the Old Testament as prefiguration of Jesus, with a focus on the prophetic nature of God's Word.
273 pp.   2013 (reprinted 2019).   w/ imprimatur.

Blessed Guilt: A Universal Conversion Story –
Extended parable on the life-giving repentance found in Jesus' blood; vaguely autobiographical but without particulars.
119 pp.   2013.   w/ imprimatur.

Chapters of the Gospels –
Exposition of the four gospels, chapter by chapter; in the style of *Our Daily Bread*.   114 pp.   2009 (reprinted 2021).   w/ imprimatur.

The Most Holy Trinity
and the Four Corners of the Universe –
A collection of writings on the Trinity and its reflection in Creation; founded upon the Shema.   300 pp. 2008. w/ imprimatur.

YHWH: Order of the Divine NAME –
On the significance of the contemplative silence that is the NAME of God, and its application to a spiritual life.   260 pp.   2008 (reprinted 2019). w/ imprimatur.

Turn of the Jubilee Year: A Conversion Song –
Autobiographical depiction of vocation search through pilgrimage to Medjugorje and stays at a hermitage or two.   230 pp.   2004.

Songs for Children of Light: Ten Albums of Lyrics –
A white on black conceptual work with simple drawings for each song. 150 pp. 2003.

silence in the city –
Short contemplative poems; moments of divine silence in the midst of city life. 148 pp. (74 pieces).   2003.

Author's Website:
www.writingsofjameskurt.org

Podcasting Site:
www.hermitinthecity.libsyn.com

www.ingramcontent.com/pod-product-compliance
Lightning Source LLC
Chambersburg PA
CBHW071452080526
44587CB00014B/2081